HOW TO THINK ABOUT GOD answers such important questions as

· Why an understanding of nuclear physics and modern cosmology actually strengthens the argument for God

· Why the best traditional argument for God fails

· How to use reason alone to form an idea of God and His nature

· Why the universe could not exist without a nurturing God

· How to bridge the gulf between reason and faith

MORTIMER J. ADLER, the originator of *Great Books of the Western World*, is a noted philosopher in his own right. He is director of the Institute for Philosophical Research, senior associate of the Aspen Institute for Humanistic Studies, author of *Philosopher at Large*, and co-author of *Great Treasury of Western Thought*.

D0683879

Bantam Books by Mortimer J. Adler

ARISTOTLE FOR EVERYBODY
HOW TO THINK ABOUT GOD

MORTIMER J. ADLER

HOW TO THINK ABOUT GOD

A Guide for the 20th-Century Pagan*

* *One who does not worship the God of Christians, Jews, or Muslims; irreligious persons*

BANTAM BOOKS
TORONTO · NEW YORK · LONDON · SYDNEY

HOW TO THINK ABOUT GOD

A Bantam Book/published by arrangement with
Macmillan Inc.

PRINTING HISTORY
Macmillan edition published March 1980
3 printings through October 1980
Bantam edition / March 1982

ISBN 0-553-20049-6

Published simultaneously in the United States and Canada

PRINTED IN THE UNITED STATES OF AMERICA

0 9 8 7 6 5 4 3 2 1

To

the memory of

ETIENNE GILSON

preceptor and friend

Contents

Contents

HOW TO THINK
ABOUT GOD

PART ONE

Prologue: About This Book and Its Author

CHAPTER 1

For Whom This Book Is Intended

THIS BOOK'S SUBTITLE STATES for whom the book is intended but, being brief, it fails to be sufficiently accurate. Although not misleading, the title does not help you to decide whether it points a finger at you.

The dictionary meaning of the word "pagan" identifies a large section of the population—all those who do not worship the God of the Christians, the Jews, or the Muslims. However, when the dictionary goes on to equate one who does not worship the God of the Christians, Jews, or Muslims with an irreligious person, it is speaking in parochial Western terms. Among the earth's population are many who do not worship the God of the Christians, Jews, and Muslims, but who are not irreligious persons.

So, to make the subtitle more precise, I should call attention to the fact that the pagans in question are the heirs of what we regard as distinctively Western civilization. They have been born and brought up in the civilization that has been the cultural environment of the three great religions of the West—Judaism, Christianity, and Islam. While living in the culture that has been the home of these three great religions, these Western pagans have chosen to remain outsiders—non-believers in and non-worshipers of the God believed in and worshiped by many of their fellow citizens. Sharing fellowship with them in the same civic and cultural community, they do not share fellowship with them in any religious community.

While the subtitle is not explicit on the point that the pagans to whom this book is addressed are *Western* men and women who do not share the religions beliefs of Judaism, Christianity, and Islam, it is explicit that they are *20th-century* men and women. Why that restrictive qualification?

In one sense, of course, the answer is obvious. There would be no point in writing a book for Western pagans of an earlier century—for persons who are not alive to be its readers. But that is not the point of stressing "20th-century" in the title. Socrates, Plato, and Aristotle, Marcus Aurelius, Epictetus, and Cicero were Western pagans. The Western peoples of pre-Christian antiquity were all pagans in the sense defined. Many remained pagans during the early centuries of the Christian era; and from the 16th century on, the number of pagans living in communities that were predominantly Christian or Muslim has steadily increased.

The number of pagans in the West today may be larger than in any previous century. It is not the number of them that matters, but their state of mind. The pagans of our day have had their minds formed by some acquaintance with 20th-century science, especially 20th-century cosmology and 20th-century subatomic physics. The cosmology and physics of classical antiquity, which provided the conceptual framework, the imagery, and the vocabulary employed by ancient pagans in their thinking about God, must be completely cast aside in any discourse about God addressed to 20th-century pagans. That conceptual framework, imagery, and vocabulary persisted throughout the Middle Ages and well into modern times; in fact, to the end of the 19th century. The cosmology of Newton as well as that of Aristotle is now completely antiquated, no longer a medium of intelligible and persuasive communication.

Not only must an effort to talk intelligibly and persuasively about God to 20th-century pagans employ an imagery and vocabulary consonant with the cosmology and physics of our day; it must also be responsive to the critical cautions that modern philosophical thought has imposed upon any discourse that attempts to be metaphysical or theological.

Modern philosophers from the time of David Hume and Immanuel Kant onward have pointed out difficulties encountered in thinking and talking about God. Their predecessors did not seem to be aware of these difficulties, but they are difficulties that can no longer be disregarded. Modern thinkers have spotted illicit steps of inference that went unnoticed in earlier centuries. They have demanded a degree of critical acumen, of subtlety, and of sophistication in the use of language not recognized by their predecessors. This is especially true of the 20th-century school of thought that goes by the name of linguistic and analytical philosophy.

The 20th-century pagans to whom this book is addressed may not be explicitly aware of these considerations, but to whatever extent their minds have been formed by what is taught in the colleges and universities of our day, either directly by undergoing such instruction, or indirectly through the popularization of such teaching, their state of mind is different from that of Western pagans in antiquity, in the Middle Ages, or even in the early centuries of the modern period.

The reader who has come this far may still feel impelled to ask whether he or she is included in the audience for whom this book is intended. Does the fact that you were willing to identify yourself as a 20th-century Western pagan automatically put you in that circle? The answer to that question is no. Does the fact that you would not so identify yourself exclude you from it? The answer to that question is also no. Those two negatives require explanation.

An eminent apologist for the Christian religion, as well as a great mathematician and experimental scientist, Blaise Pascal, helps to provide the needed explanation. He divided all mankind into three groups. In his view, these comprised:

1. Those who know God and love him
2. Those who do not know God but seek him
3. Those who neither know God nor seek him

Clearly, persons in the first of the three groups are not pagans; they may be either religious Christians, religious Jews, or religious Muslims. They are persons who believe in God and participate in the worship of him. Persons in the second and third group do not believe in the God worshiped by religious Christians, Jews, and Muslims. By that negative criterion, they are all pagans, but with this important difference: Persons in the second of Pascal's groups, while not believing in God, are openminded pagans—at least to the extent of their being willing to consider the question whether God exists. Those in the third group are resolutely committed pagans, as resolutely committed as are the religious persons in the first of Pascal's group.

It would be folly to address a discussion of God to such resolutely committed pagans—persons who not only disbelieve in the existence of God but who have also closed their minds on the subject; and who for one reason or another have no interest in the question whether God exists and are, therefore, unwilling to devote any time or effort to the consideration of such matters. They are the 20th-century pagans for whom this book is *not* intended.

Is it intended, then, only for the 20th-century pagans who fall into Pascal's second division? Only for those who are not religious Jews, Christians, or Muslims, but who, at the same time, have some residual curiosity about the God in whom many of their fellow citizens believe? Precisely because of that lurking curiosity, which underlies their interest in the question of God's existence, and their willingness to make some effort to consider it, this book is addressed to them. They—the openminded pagans of our day and of our culture—constitute the primary audience for which it is written.

But it is not only for them. The non-pagans who belong in Pascal's first division may also find this book of some interest, not all of them, perhaps, but certainly some—those who would say that some of their best friends are pagans and who would, therefore, be interested in learning how their pagan friends might be persuaded that God exists. They are not the audience to whom this book is primarily addressed, for they are not persons to be persuaded. They are already convinced and committed. Nevertheless, they may learn something about the underpinnings of their own belief by following the steps to be undertaken in the process of persuading their pagan friends whose minds still remain open.

CHAPTER 2

What Readers Can Expect from This Book

"THEOLOGY" IS THE NAME for thinking about God. In the tradition of Western civilization, such thinking began with the ancient Greeks. It is to be found in the philosophical writings of Plato and Aristotle, dating from the 5th and 4th centuries B.C.

Though the popular religion of the ancient Greek cities was polytheistic, devoted to the worship of many divinities, the Greek equivalent of the word "God" was used by Plato and Aristotle in the singular and with a capital letter—by Plato in the tenth book of his dialogue, *The Laws;* by Aristotle in the eighth book of his *Physics* and the twelfth book of a work that has come to be called his *Metaphysics.* In all three texts, the conclusion reached by purely philosophical thought is an affirmation of God's existence. In the *Physics,* Aristotle comes to this conclusion in the context of thinking about the physical universe as a whole; in the *Meta-physics*, in the context of thinking about the diverse ways in which things can be said to exist.

Plato's and Aristotle's thinking about God was doubly pagan. Not only was it unaffected by the religious beliefs of the ancient Jews, with which these Greek thinkers seem to have been unacquainted; it was also unaffected by the popular religious beliefs of their fellow citizens. For these reasons, calling it "pagan" is equivalent to saying that it was purely philosophical thinking about God.

The one point of resemblance between Plato's and Aristotle's books about God and the books of the Old Testament lies in their monotheism. In all other respects, they are almost totally dissimilar. Regarded by the ancient Jews as Sacred Scripture, as writing inspired by God revealing himself to man, the books of the Old Testament do not contain man's philosophical thinking about God. If philosophical thinking about God is theological, then the books of the Old Testament are not theological books, even though they are replete with references to God.

I say all this to make clear what readers can expect to find in this book—purely philosophical thinking about God, which aims to discover and to assess whatever reasons can be found for affirming that God exists, as Plato and Aristotle affirmed God's existence many centuries ago. Like their books about God, this too is a theological book. In the sense in which their thinking about God was pagan (unaffected by current religious beliefs), this book, intended for 20th-century pagans, aims to engage in thinking about God that is not only philosophical but also pagan.

What has happened in the twenty-five centuries that have elapsed since the time of Plato and Aristotle makes the fore-going characterization of this book's aim not as simple or plain as it might at first appear to be. This is a theological book, but not in the sense in which the *Summa Theologica,* written by Thomas Aquinas in the 13th century, is theological. That work in Christian theology is a systematic exposition of the articles of Christian faith, an explanation of Christian beliefs about God, both in himself and in his relation to creatures.

A little earlier, similar works were written by the great Jewish theologian Moses Maimonides and by the great Muslim theologian Avicenna, both of whom influenced Aquinas. All three were influenced by Aristotle's philosophical thought about God as well as by the Sacred Scriptures which they respectively believed to be the revealed word of God.

Though philosophical thought entered into the writing of these great theological works in the 12th and 13th centuries, they were primarily and predominantly controlled by the Sacred Scriptures in which their writers believed and from which they derived their religious beliefs—their articles of religious faith. That is why such works are appropriately described as works of *sacred* theology. They were not written by pagans nor were they intended for pagans.

A somewhat different kind of theological writing emerged in the 12th and 13th centuries. Another great Arabic thinker, Averroës, tried to write a purely philosophical book about God. It was written in response to a book by al-Ghazali, entitled *The Destruction of Philosophy*, which attempted to defend the purity of the Islamic faith from the incursions of philosophical thought. The response was entitled *The Destruction of the Destruction.* Though Averroës relied heavily upon what he had learned from Aristotle, he was not a pagan, nor was his book written for pagans, but for those who, like himself, participated in the religious community of Islam.

In addition to writing the *Summa Theologica*, avowedly a work in sacred theology, Thomas Aquinas wrote another large treatise entitled *Summa Contra Gentiles*. It was intended for "unbelievers," specifically for the Moors and Jews in Spain, who were "unbelievers" or "infidels" only in the sense that they did not believe in the divinity of Jesus Christ. They could hardly be called "unbelievers" without qualification, since they shared with Aquinas the religious belief that the books of the Old Testament were the revealed word of God, the God worshiped in all three religious communities—that of Judaism and of Islam as well as that of Christianity. The gentiles to whom Aquinas addressed his work were hardly pagans in the sense that Plato and Aristotle were pagans.

The Destruction of the Destruction, written by Averroës in the 12th century, and the *Summa Contra Gentiles,* written by Aquinas in the 13th century, came to be called works in "natural theology" rather than works in "sacred theology" because they tried to derive their controlling principles from reason rather than from religious faith. To the extent that they succeeded in this effort, these works represent philosophical thinking about God. But neither Averroës nor Aquinas was explicitly aware of how much their philosophical thinking was imbued with Islamic or Christian religious beliefs.

While both were disciples of Aristotle, neither understood or recognized the difference between their state of mind when they tried to engage in philosophical thought about God and Aristotle's state of mind four centuries before the advent of Christianity and ten centuries before the advent of Islam. Their religious beliefs colored, directed, and controlled their philosophical thinking about God in spite of all their efforts to appeal to reason alone. The reason they employed was not the pagan reason of Aristotle, but reason altered—or, as it is sometimes said, elevated and illuminated—by the light of their religious faith. Hence their so-called natural theology was not *purely* philosophical thinking about God, thinking unaffected by any religious beliefs whatsoever.

What I have just said about the natural theology of Averroës and Aquinas applies also to the natural theology we find in the writings of such eminent 17th- and 18th-century philosophers as Descartes and Leibnitz. Both were men of Christian faith. The philosophical thinking of both was profoundly affected by that faith; and so their contribution to natural theology did not represent purely philosophical thinking about God. It was not written by pagans, nor intended primarily for pagans.

Since the 17th and 18th centuries, innumerable works in natural theology have been published, written in the main by men of Christian faith and intended for their fellow Christians. What characterizes all of them, as what characterized the earlier works of Averroës, Aquinas, Descartes, and Leibnitz, is their claim to affirm the existence of God on the basis of reason alone—reason totally unaided, unaffected, and above all unenlightened by religious beliefs.

As I have already said, that claim is, in my judgment, invalid. At least, it is exaggerated. Moreover, if the term "natural theology" is properly applied to such works, to distinguish them from works in "sacred theology" which do not claim to be based on reason alone, then I must discard the term "natural theology" as inapplicable to my own work.

The book I am writing is not a work in natural theology, because natural theology as it has been developed in the West since the beginning of the Christian era has not been written by pagans for pagans. Since this book will try to do what natural theologians so far have not done (base its thinking about God on reason alone, unaffected by Western religious beliefs), it should perhaps be described as a work in "philosophical" rather than in "natural" theology.

During the modern period, from the 18th century on and especially in our own time, a great deal of philosophical thinking about God has been done, the main thrust of which has been severe criticism of the reasoning to be found in

Christian natural theology, leading to rejection of the claim made by natural theologians that the existence of God can be affirmed on the basis of reason alone. There is no question that such books, adversely critical of the thinking done and the conclusions reached by natural theologians, are purely philosophical works; but since they reject the claim that tenable reasons can be found for affirming God's existence, they might be more appropriately described as anti-theological rather than as theological works.

This book will, I hope, turn out to be not only purely philosophical but also affirmatively theological rather than anti-theological. That, in brief, is what the reader can expect from this book, neither more nor less. Its closest affinity is with Aristotle's philosophical thinking about God, but coming twenty-five centuries later, it cannot help being affected by all the thinking about God that has occurred in the intervening centuries.

I have in mind not only the thinking done in Western sacred theology and in Western natural theology, but also the modern and recent philosophical thinking that I have described as anti-theological. In addition, as I remarked in the preceding chapter, a book intended for 20th-century pagans must be couched in terms that reflect 20th-century science, especially its subatomic physics and its cosmology. In this respect, it will have little resemblance to Aristotle's thinking and writing about God.

Having now clarified the character of this book in relation to other kinds of writing about God, there are a number of points I would like to comment on briefly because I think they will be helpful to the reader. They should at least safeguard him or her against certain misunderstandings.

First of all, it must be pointed out that if this book fails to uncover tenable reasons for affirming God's existence, such failure does not mean (a) that God's existence is *disproved*, (b) that God's existence *cannot be proved*, (c) that it is *in-*

correct to think that God exists, or (d) that it is *erroneous* to believe that God exists. Failure to prove God's existence concerns only the reasonableness of belief in God. Belief in God may be unreasonable without thereby being false.

Religious persons in the Middle Ages repeatedly said "*Credo nisi absurdum est*" (I believe even though it is absurd, that is, unreasonable), or "*Credo quia absurdum est*" (I believe because it is absurd). Another mediaeval maxim—faith seeking understanding—presents the other face of the relation between faith and reason. Resting on articles of faith as its basic premises, sacred theology undertakes to do all it can to make what faith affirms as intelligible and as reasonable as possible.

When we use such epithets as "atheist" and "agnostic," we are referring in the first instance to a person who denies God's existence or disbelieves in God without disproving God's existence; and in the second instance, to a person who, whether or not believing in God, maintains that God's existence can be affirmed by religious faith alone, and not by reason.

This calls for some comment on the distinction between "knowledge" and "belief." When we understand the demonstration of a conclusion in mathematics, we say that we know that conclusion to be true, not that we believe in it. Only persons who do not understand the truth that two plus two equals four or that all right angles are equal would be compelled to say that they believe rather than know these mathematical propositions to be true. They may hold such beliefs on the authority of their teacher or their textbook, but without understanding what makes the proposition true, they cannot say that they know it.

Similarly, when we understand the grounds for affirming a conclusion of experimental or empirical science, we can say that we know it rather than that we believe it to be true. Though the word "know" has a somewhat different connotation when we apply it to a conclusion of experimental or empirical science, as contrasted with a conclusion demonstrated by mathematical reasoning, it is nevertheless the right word to use rather than "believe." Only persons who adopt a scientific conclusion solely on the authority of someone else (without any understanding of the evidence and reasoning that supports it) should say that they believe rather than know its truth.

When we come to thinking about God, especially about God's existence, the word "know," as applied to conclusions demonstrated in mathematics or to scientific conclusions established experimentally or empirically, may require more certitude than is attainable. Hence it may be necessary to use the word "believe" with certain qualifications attached to it.

In the preceding pages, religious belief has been repeatedly referred to. It has also been said that purely philosophical thinking about God should be unaffected by religious beliefs, the articles of a creed that is affirmed respectively by religious Jews, Christians, or Muslims, and affirmed as a matter of faith on their part, not as the result of argument, reasoning, or inferences of any sort.

If argument, reasoning, or inference leads us to affirm the existence of God because we have thereby found tenable reasons for doing so, should we say that we know that God exists or that we believe it? If the tenable reasons we have found fall short of the degree of certitude that justifies us in using the word "know" for mathematically demonstrated and empirically established truths, then we must have recourse to the word "believe," always remembering to add the qualification that the belief we have adopted differs from religious belief in that the truth thus affirmed is affirmed on the basis of reason alone. This is not to say that religious beliefs are ipso facto unreasonable, but only that they are not based on reason alone and that they may be adopted even if they are unreasonable. The whole concern of a purely philosophical theology is with the reasonableness of the belief that God exists.

A third point to be noted follows directly on what has just been said. In the three monotheistic religions of the West—Judaism, Christianity, and Islam—the proposition that God exists is *not* an article of faith or religious belief. The first article of faith in all three religions is that God has revealed himself to us in Holy Writ or Sacred Scripture. This, of course, entails the affirmation that the God who has revealed himself exists. But it goes far beyond that proposition to something that can never be proved, or even argued about, something that is always and only an article of faith or religious belief: namely, the fact of Divine revelation.

In the opening pages of the *Summa Theologica*, Aquinas pointed out that the proposition "God exists" is a *preamble* to faith, not an *article* of faith. As a preamble to faith, it is something for philosophers to think about. Those who are not able or who do not wish to think about the existence of God can, of course, affirm the proposition "God exists" as a matter of religious belief, consequent upon the prior affirmation by faith, and by faith alone, that God has revealed himself to us in Sacred Scripture.

It is in no way improper to argue about whether belief in God's existence can be established by reason alone, or at least thereby made reasonable. But it would be quite improper to argue about the reasonableness of the first article of religious faith, that Sacred Scripture represents God's revelation of himself to us. That belief can be neither proved nor disproved, nor is it really a proper subject of argument pro and con.

Finally, a word to the reader about the course of the discussion in the chapters to follow. The following chapter concludes the Prologue. Part Two is concerned with errors to be avoided in any thinking about God that aims to be purely philosophical and to avoid coloration or direction from religious beliefs. Part Three then sets the stage for constructing philosophical arguments for the reasonableness of belief in the existence of God. It does so by paying special attention to the uniqueness of the word "God" as a name, the meaning of which we must establish, and to the uniqueness of the proposition "God exists" as a proposition to be affirmed by reason and by reason alone.

With the stage set, Part Four offers the best of the traditional arguments for belief in the existence of God, and explains not only why it is the best, but also why it fails. That having been done, Part Five takes account of the stumbling block that was not surmounted by the best of the traditional arguments and then advances an argument that appears to avoid the pitfalls that beset other arguments.

Finally, in Part Six, as an Epilogue, we are concerned with the severe limits of philosophical thinking about God and, therefore, with the question of its significance, especially in relation to Western religious beliefs that this purely pagan approach has tried to keep from intruding up to this point.

CHAPTER 3

What Readers Should Know About the Author

THE READER WILL, I think, soon see why I deem it appropriate to say something about myself as background relevant to understanding this book.

I was born of Jewish parents. Only my father was religiously orthodox, but he was also religiously tolerant. He did not try to impose his orthodoxy upon my mother who, with my grandmother, worshiped in what was then called a reform synagogue, the Sunday school of which I attended in my early years. I also attended religious services on the Sabbath with my mother and grandmother, and became acquainted with the liturgy—the chants and prayers, especially the Kaddish, or prayer for the dead, and the readings from the Torah.

My Sunday-school attendance terminated with participation in a confirmation class and in the ceremony of confirmation. Shortly after that, impelled by adolescent rebelliousness, I fell away from religious observance and became, as was characteristic of my age, a scoffer to the point of impiety. My parents were indulgent, requiring little more than my being respectful of their feelings in public.

Since my youth I have had little or no involvement in the ceremonies and practices of the Jewish religion or in Jewish religious life. In later years, through marriage, I have become involved in the religious life of my family, at least to the extent of frequently attending, with my wife and children, Sunday services in a Protestant Episcopal church and becoming acquainted with its liturgy, its Thirty-nine Articles, and its Book of Common Prayer. There have been moments in my life, during my late thirties and early forties and later in my early sixties, when I contemplated becoming a Christian—in the first instance a Roman Catholic, in the second an Episcopalian. Suffice it to say, I have not done so. I have remained the pagan that I became when I fell away from the religion of my parents.

From what I have said so far, readers for whom this book is primarily intended will perceive that I am akin to them— a 20th-century pagan, nurtured in the civilization of the West. That is as it should be. A book about God written for pagans should be written by a pagan but, it should also be added, by one who, while still a pagan, is deeply concerned with the question of God's existence and with trying to establish the reasonableness of belief in God.

That I am. In sharp contrast to the superficiality of my involvement in religious worship, Jewish or Christian, is my intense, profound, and lifelong involvement in the study of theology. It began in the early 1920s, when, as an undergraduate at Columbia University, I first read Aristotle's *Metaphysics* and became fascinated with the argument for God's existence in Book XII. Shortly afterward, in 1923, the year after I was graduated from college and became a member of the Columbia faculty assigned to teach, with Mark Van Doren, a section of the course devoted to reading the great books, I first discovered the *Summa Theologica* of Thomas Aquinas. Since then, for almost sixty years, theology—first sacred, then natural, and finally purely philosophical theology as well as anti-theological philosophy—has been a subject of consuming interest in my life. In that respect, as the pagan author of this book I am probably different from most of its pagan readers.

When John Erskine made up the list of great books that became the assigned reading in the honors course at Columbia, called "Classics of the Western World," the only work by Thomas Aquinas with which he was then acquainted— or the only one that he thought was readily available—consisted in the translation of the *Summa Contra Gentiles* by Father Rickaby. He selected a series of chapters from that work dealing with human happiness, on earth and hereafter.

The intellectual tenor and style of Aquinas caught my fancy and I wanted to read more than the assigned chapters; but, so far as I could tell, there were no works by Thomas Aquinas in the Columbia library, at least not in English. Fortunately, a friend of mine, Richard McKeon, had just returned to Columbia from studying at the Sorbonne with Etienne Gilson, the eminent historian of mediaeval philosophy. McKeon told me that the entire *Summa Theologica* had been translated into English by the Dominican Fathers, had been published by Benziger Brothers, and could be purchased at their bookstore in downtown Manhattan.

Down I went one Saturday morning and found twenty-one or twenty-two relatively slender volumes of the *Summa* on the shelf. Volume one, I discovered, contained that portion of the *Summa* entitled "Treatise on God." Purchasing it, I returned to my quarters, where I was joined by two friends who shared my interest in Aquinas. One of them, Scott Buchanan, who had received his doctorate from Harvard and had been a Rhodes Scholar at Oxford, had never seen a page of Aquinas. Mediaeval theology in general and Aquinas in particular had not surfaced at the prestigious institutions in which his mind had been cultivated. The other friend, Arthur Rubin, much more involved in Jewish religious life than I, and much more inclined toward piety, had some acquaintance with the thought of Moses Maimonides, the Jewish predecessor of Aquinas. Both Scott and Arthur had philosophical bents of mind that predisposed them to be interested in philosophical speculations about God.

That Saturday morning, for some reason that I cannot recall, we did not begin our reading of the *Summa* with the question about God's existence, but rather with questions about God's nature, the first of which was "Whether God has a body." As in the treatment of each of the thousand or more questions that comprise the *Summa*, Aquinas begins with a statement of objections to the answer that he himself defends, in this case a negative answer to the question. The opening sentence in Objection 1 reads: "It seems that God has a body."

Both Arthur and Scott were overcome by the simplicity and elegance of that statement, and by the highly cogent reasoning which Aquinas advanced in support of a proposition that he regarded as false. I must confess that, in the series of Saturday-morning sessions which followed, our fascination with the dialectics of objections advanced and rebutted in the treatment of questions about God's nature overshadowed our interest in the truth or falsity of what we were reading. In any case, we did not then pay much attention to the question about God's existence—Question 2— which we had skipped over.

That, for me, came later. In the early thirties, after Robert Hutchins became president of the University of Chicago, he invited me to join him there and decided that he and I would introduce the reading of the great books into the curriculum

by teaching a two-year seminar for freshmen and sopho-
mores. At my suggestion, the "Treatise on God" from the
Summa Theologica of Aquinas was placed on the list of assigned readings. Hutchins, having been a student at Oberlin,
a graduate of Yale, and a dean of its law school, had never
heard of Aquinas; but, having been brought up in the home
of a Protestant clergyman, he did have an interest in theology.

I read and reread the "Treatise on God" many times with
students in the great-books seminar that Hutchins and I conducted over a period of fifteen years. My interest focused
more and more on the question of God's existence as discussed in Question 2, and on the five attempts, advanced by
Aquinas, to demonstrate the truth of the proposition "God
exists."

In those years I was persuaded that Aquinas, by reason
alone and without any insight derived from religious beliefs
or dogmas, had succeeded in proving God's existence. As I
look back at it now, I realize that I had little or no understanding of the philosophical problems involved in any attempt by reason alone to prove God's existence. I had little
or no understanding of the difficulties that must be faced and
overcome in order to set the stage for attempting to formulate, without any light drawn from religious beliefs, an
argument that might show the reasonableness of a purely
secular, or pagan, belief in God.

As a consequence of my lack of understanding at that
time, I was guilty of misleading the students in a succession
of classes, students whom I tried to persuade that Aquinas
had done the job. Some of them, I am delighted to recall,
stoutly and stalwartly resisted my efforts. One in particular
I remember. He was a student in a special seminar conducted
for those planning to enter law school. One year—in 1936,
I believe—that seminar began with the "Treatise on God."
I announced that I would not move a page beyond Question 2 until I had succeeded in persuading every member

of the class that the existence of God could be demonstrated by one or another of the proofs advanced by Aquinas. One by one they gave in, either from some measure of conviction or, more likely, from weariness and boredom with the protracted process; but one, Charles Adams, indomitably held out.

Finally, my professorial colleague, Malcolm Sharp, called a halt to the proceedings and suggested that, instead of sticking to my guns with Adams, I tell the class about the life and work of Aquinas. I did so, stressing the shortness of his career as a teacher and writer (a little more than twenty years) in which, under the austerities of monastic life, with no libraries, typewriters, or other facilities, he produced a series of works which, in ordinary-size volumes, would occupy many shelves; and, I added, most of these works were filled with quotations from Sacred Scripture, from the philosophers of antiquity, from the Fathers of the Church, and from his immediate predecessors in the 11th and 12th centuries—all this without having the convenience of a well-stocked library or an adequate filing system.

When I had finished, Adams spoke up. He rebuked me for not having started out by telling the class what I had just finished reporting. "Why?" I asked. "Because," said Adams, "if you had told us all this about Aquinas, you would not have had to bother our minds with arguments about God's existence. Aquinas could not have done what he did without God's help."

It was not until 1943 that I made some progress in my understanding of the problem and corrected the errors of my earlier teaching. The occasion was the sixtieth birthday of Jacques Maritain, the French Catholic philosopher who was then one of the most eminent disciples of Thomas Aquinas and a leader in the movement known as "neo-Thomism." Having been invited by Hutchins some years earlier to come annually to the University of Chicago as a visiting lecturer, he had also become a close personal friend of mine. On the occasion of Maritain's sixtieth birthday, *The Thomist*, a philosophical and theological journal devoted to the thought of Aquinas, decided to publish an anniversary volume and invited me to contribute to it. I elected to submit an essay entitled "The Demonstration of God's Existence."

The main points that I tried to defend in that essay were as follows: (1) that Aristotle had not succeeded in proving God's existence; (2) that Aquinas, relying too heavily upon Aristotle, in Question 2 of the *Summa*, had also failed; (3) that none of his five ways offered a correct approach to the problem of proving God's existence; (4) that one difficulty which Aquinas could not overcome in writing the *Summa Theologica*, a work in sacred, not natural, theology, resided in the fact that the order of exposition imposed upon him by the demands of sacred theology placed much too early—in Question 2—the consideration of arguments for God's existence, whereas, if one were proceeding philosophically, as one should in natural theology, there would be extensive intellectual preparation for considering the question, and only at the very end would one attempt to advance an argument that might be probative; (5) that, although Aquinas failed to prove God's existence in Question 2, one could find in later treatises of Part One of the *Summa*, especially the treatises on creation, on the work of the six days of genesis, and on the divine government of the universe, extraordinary insights that might be employed to construct a better argument for God's existence than the five ways presented in Question 2; (6) that one such argument would be better than two or more, for the reasoning should be as simple and elegant as possible, and a multiplicity of arguments betrayed weakness rather than strength.

Having supported all these points as cogently as I could, with ample documentation from relevant texts in the *Summa* of Aquinas and in the writings of his disciples, I then proceeded to construct an argument for God's existence based on the insights I had derived from my study of the whole of Part One of the *Summa*.

After presenting the argument, I called attention to a number of difficulties which it failed to overcome and which, at the time, I could not see how to overcome. I concluded by saying that I thought further work along these lines might remove the difficulties. Until that occurred, I would have to say that God's existence might be proved in the future, but that it had not yet been proved.

The editors of *The Thomist* were appalled by my temerity. They were so upset, in fact, that one of them phoned me to say that they could not publish my essay because it contradicted a declared dogma of the Church. When I asked which dogma, I was told that it had been declared, as an article of the Roman Catholic faith, that God's existence could be demonstrated by reason and by reason alone. I had not contradicted that dogma, I replied. I had not said that God's existence could not be proved by reason; I had said only that Aquinas had not done it. It could hardly be a dogma of the Church that, as a matter of historical fact, Aquinas had succeeded in demonstrating God's existence in the 13th century.

My response brought the editors to their senses. My essay was published and met with a totally adverse reception from many quarters, including long letters from Jacques Maritain, trying to make me see the fundamental error or errors I had committed. Subsequently, in a book entitled *Approaches to God*, he ignored my replies to his letters, in which I tried to point out that what he regarded as my errors were in fact steps that I had found it necessary to introduce in order to correct the errors in the traditional approach to the problem of proving God's existence. I had not succeeded in changing his mind the least bit. A footnote in that book cautioned the reader against adopting the approach I had urged in my essay for *The Thomist*.

From 1945 until the publication of *Great Books of the Western World* and the *Syntopicon* in 1952, I was so busily engaged in editorial work on that project that my preoccupation with the question of God's existence temporarily lapsed. Subsequently, however, in the middle fifties and throughout the sixties, I returned to the subject, and found numerous occasions to deliver a lecture on it, both to popular and to academic audiences. I rewrote that lecture each time I gave it, trying each time to improve the preparation for the argument and to tighten the argument itself. Nevertheless, that lecture in its final stages still left me with unsurmounted difficulties—with stumbling blocks I could not get over and pitfalls I could not avoid. I found it necessary to confess, in conclusion, that I had not yet succeeded in doing what I felt philosophical thought by itself should be able to do.

If I had not finally been able to go beyond that lecture at its best, I would not have undertaken to write this book. It is only in the last few years that I have gained the confidence needed to do so—confidence that I can at last present an argument that might be persuasive to 20th-century pagans. That assurance has come from a number of sources.

One has been my study of modern anti-theological philosophical literature—the criticisms of traditional natural theology written by philosophers since the 18th century and especially in our own time. I realized that these criticisms did not apply to the argument which had been slowly forming in my mind, however applicable they may be to the traditional natural theology that is essentially Christian, and so not purely philosophical, in its tenets and its temper.

Another source has been my growing realization that the main attacks directed against traditional arguments for God's existence, especially those regarded by contemporary ana-

lytical and linguistic philosophy as most trenchant and devastating, misfire completely. They do not hit home because,
while forged with great logical sophistication and acumen,
they spring from either no understanding or insufficient understanding of the metaphysical points involved in the argument. My recognition of this deficiency and its consequences was reinforced by reading Edward Sillem's *Ways
of Thinking About God*, in which Chapter 7 is a seventy-
page-long dialogue between Thomas Aquinas and some
modern critics of the argument for God's existence.

Still another source has been my careful reading of two
books by Etienne Gilson—*Christianity and Philosophy* and
Being and Some Philosophers. From them I have learned that
Aquinas did not know about himself what it took Gilson
years of study to discover about him: namely, that his
philosophical thinking was Christian, not Aristotelian or pagan, and that when he engaged in what he himself would
have regarded as natural rather than sacred theology, the
operation of his mind was deeply affected by his religious
faith and so was not purely philosophical. His thinking about
God was directed and controlled by an understanding of
God that he had acquired from his religious faith, not from
philosophical speculation. Obviously, an understanding that
depends on faith cannot be communicated to those devoid
of it.

I also learned from Gilson that in modern times, philosophical thinking about God has split in two directions: on
the one hand, there is the direction taken by those who,
being men of religious faith like Aquinas, made contributions
to a natural theology that was not purely philosophical or
pagan; on the other hand, there is the direction taken by
those who, being men devoid of religious faith, criticized
and rejected a natural theology that they quite rightly sus-
pected of not being purely philosophical. The first group affirmed God's existence and some of them even regarded it

as demonstrable with certitude. Rejecting that claim, the second group went further and denied that reasonable grounds could be found for believing in God.

This picture presented a challenge to me. Could I reach an affirmative conclusion about the possibility of discovering reasonable grounds for believing in God, yet, at the same time, do so in a purely philosophical or thoroughly pagan fashion? And could I do so in the light of the findings and formulations of 20th-century science? Since my answer to these questions is positive, I have at last overcome my reluctance to write this book.

I now have a measure of confidence that I may be able to persuade some of my readers who are fellow pagans. But what about those other readers, those persons of religious faith whose interest in this book lies in the fact that they have friends who are pagans and who might become religious if they were persuaded that belief in God can be made reasonable?

They may think, not without reason, that only God, as understood and affirmed by theologians who are also men of religious faith, is the deity whom they can worship; whereas God, as understood and affirmed by a purely philosophical or pagan theologian, cannot possibly evoke a truly religious response. They may be right.

The God that is the object of pagan philosophical thought is not the God of Abraham, Isaac, and Jacob, or of Moses, Jesus, and Mohammed. However, there may be some bridge from one to the other. Whether there is or not remains to be seen.

PART TWO

Errors to Be Avoided

CHAPTER 4

World Without Beginning or End

DID THE WORLD—the universe, the cosmos as a whole—have a beginning and will it come to an end, or did the world always exist and will it always continue in existence, a world without beginning or end?

How this question is answered has a direct and critical bearing on any attempt to argue for God's existence. Where should we go in search of an answer? To religion? To science? To philosophy? I suggest that we consult all three and then decide which answer we must adopt for the purpose of a pagan and purely philosophical inquiry into the question of God's existence.

In our Western tradition, men of religious faith—that of Judaism, Christianity, and Islam—all give the same answer, the answer they find in the opening line of Genesis, the first book of the Old Testament: "In the beginning God created heaven and earth." When they affirm, as they do, that the world had a beginning, they do so on what is, for them, the highest possible warrant—the word of God himself as it is revealed to them in Holy Writ.

In the science of the 20th century, two rival astronomical or cosmological theories claim our attention. One is the *steady state* theory; the other, the *big bang* theory.

According to the steady state theory, the cosmos has always existed and will always exist and, at any time, the universe is everywhere in a uniform condition. This theory has now been generally discredited by well-established evidence that the universe is constantly expanding, the galaxies moving apart at increasing velocity. However, the steady state theory did include one point on which I will comment presently. It held that the steady state of the universe is maintained by the continuous "creation"—or coming into existence out of nothing—of hydrogen nuclei.

The big bang theory, which is now regnant, would appear to give the opposite answer. Popularizations of this theory have recently appeared in books entitled *The First Three Minutes* and *God and the Astronomers*. According to this theory, somewhere between fifteen and twenty billion years ago, the world began with an explosion of cosmic dimensions. The world has been steadily running down since then, and it will eventually come to a halt in what is sometimes called a "thermodynamic death"—the ultimate entropy of matter and energy so degraded that nothing further can happen.

The scientists who discuss the evidence for this theory are precise in their handling of the astronomical observations—the phenomena and the measurements—that relate to their hypothesis. Unfortunately, they are not equally precise in their handling of such words as "beginning" and "end." When they speak of the world's having a beginning, do they mean (a) that the observable cosmos as we know it and as it has developed up to the present moment came into existence at a prior time which we can estimate as being so many billion years ago; or do they mean (b) that the cosmos came into existence out of nothing so many billion years ago, before which time nothing existed? An examination of the most carefully written scientific treatments of the astronomical evidence, and of the cosmological theory which appears to fit that evidence, will discover that the big bang theory does not posit an absolute beginning of the cosmos— a coming into existence out of nothing—but only an initial event in the development of the cosmos as we now know it, an event that occurred at a time that is estimated as between fifteen and twenty billion years ago.

The most important point to note is one that careful expositions of current cosmological speculation make clear. Our present techniques of observation and measurement, and the technical facilities they employ, do not permit us to penetrate the past beyond the time, some fifteen to twenty billion years ago, when the big bang occurred.

What is being said here is not that past time is limited (finite rather than infinite), but only that our knowledge of past time is limited—limited to a time beyond which our observations and measurements cannot go. Time may extend back infinitely beyond that initial explosion of matter, out of which the present shape of the cosmos has developed, but unless some radical alteration in our techniques and instruments of observation and measurement occurs, we will never be able to penetrate the veil that hides that infinite past from us.

Similarly, when the scientists tell us that the cosmos in its present shape has developed over a period of from fifteen to twenty billion years from a state of matter and energy that then underwent a cosmic convulsion, what is being said is *not* that nothing existed before that event. Obviously something did exist before that event, for otherwise there would have been nothing to explode and start the universe (as we know it) off on the course of its development. The fact that the cosmos, as we now know it, began to develop then does not mean that nothing existed before that development started. Science may never be able to tell us about the state of the cosmos in the time before that event. We are hardly justified in interpreting the silence of science as a negative answer to questions about the pre-existence of the cosmos.

I said earlier that I would return to one point involved in the now discredited steady state theory of the cosmos. The scientific exponents of this hypothesis incautiously permitted themselves to speak of "the continuous creation of matter," by which they appear to mean that, at all moments of time, hydrogen nuclei come into existence out of nothing.

Permit me now to introduce what at first may strike the reader as a strange word. A moment's further consideration will lead the reader to realize that it is not so strange after all, since a related word, having the opposite meaning, is current in everyone's daily vocabulary. That related word is "annihilation." All of us speak of things being annihilated, though we do so somewhat loosely, because we really mean that they have perished or disappeared rather than that they have been totally annihilated.

In any case, the strange word that I wish to introduce is "exnihilation," the very opposite in meaning to "annihilation." Something is exnihilated if it comes into existence *out of* nothing, just as something is annihilated if it passes out of existence *into* nothing. The birth of a living organism is not an exnihilation, for the progeny came into existence out of something, not nothing. Similarly, the death of a living organism is not an annihilation, for though that particular individual has ceased to be, its perishing does not involve its passing out of existence into nothing. Its decaying flesh may be eaten by another organism; its bones may be buried; its ashes may be scattered to the wind. It has not been reduced to nothing.

We shall find that these two words—"exhinilation" and "annihilation"—will have critical significance in much of the discussion that lies ahead of us in subsequent chapters. We cannot get along without them. However, for our present purposes, I have introduced them only to say that when scientists talk about the beginning of the world in an initial explosion of matter and energy, they are not talking about its exhinilation; nor, when they refer to the end of the world in a thermodynamic slowdown or death, are they talking about its annihilation. If by "beginning" and "end" we mean a beginning that is an exhinilation of the cosmos and an end that is its annihilation, then science cannot now give us an answer, and probably never will be able to give us an answer, to the question whether the world has a beginning and an end.

Before I turn to philosophy for an answer, let me comment in passing on a curious quirk of the scientific mind. When they consider the implications of the big bang theory, astronomers and cosmologists, we are told, shy away from it, not on scientific grounds, but because they—or some of them at least—fear that it lends confirmation to the religious belief that God exists as the creator of a universe that had a beginning. They fail to understand that "to create," in the strict theological sense of that term, is "to exhinilate."

As we observed a moment ago, the big bang may be the beginning of the cosmos as we now know it and as it has developed since that initial event beyond which we cannot penetrate into the past, but it is not the exhinilation or creation of the cosmos. Yet, if science finally adopts the big bang theory as the hypothesis most consonant with all the evidence, it will not have given any aid or comfort to Western religious belief, which understands the opening words of

Genesis to mean that the cosmos began when it was exnihilated by God, before which event God existed but nothing else did.

The steady state theory, if it had been adopted by science, would have put science and religion into bed together,
as strange bedfellows, indeed! If that hypothesis really as-
serted what it appeared to assert, namely, that units of matter (hydrogen nuclei) continually come into existence out
of nothing, then that continuous exnihilation or creation of
matter would require us to presuppose the existence of a
creative agency. Those scientists who do not wish to give
aid or comfort to religion should, therefore, have shied away
from the steady state hypothesis, not from the big bang hypothesis, even if the former had been more tenable in the
light of all the evidence.

The steady state theory would not have lent support to
the statement in Genesis that *"In the beginning,* God created
heaven and earth," for it holds that matter is being created
continuously throughout time, not just at an initial instant.
However, if creation or exnihilation, whether at an initial
instant or throughout time, were to be affirmed by science,
that would require us to affirm also the existence of a creator
or exnihilator—the agency to which Western religions give
the name "God."

Let us turn now to philosophy for an answer to our question about the world's beginning and end. Here we find opposite views. On the one hand, we have Aristotle and his
mediaeval Arabic disciple, Averroës, arguing for the proposition that the universe is eternal or everlasting, without beginning or end. Time is infinite, going backward to no first
instant and going forward to no last; and in that infinite or
endless time, motion or change occurs everlastingly.

In the 13th century, Aquinas disputed this view with
Christian followers of Averroës. In a famous disputation at
the University of Paris, the written record of which comes

down to us under the title "Disputed Questions about the Eternity of the World," Aquinas rejected the authority of Aristotle and the defense of Aristotle by Averroës, for two reasons, not one.

As a Christian theologian, he rejected the Aristotelian and Averroistic position simply because it was contrary to his Christian faith; more specifically, that article of his Christian faith which rests on affirming the truth of the first sentence in Genesis.

However, Aquinas did not stop there. As a philosopher, quite apart from his religious belief that the world had come into existence out of nothing by Divine creation, a supernatural act not a natural event, Aquinas took and brilliantly defended the position that philosophical reasoning, in the light of everything we can know about the universe, will never be able to *prove* either that the world had a beginning or that it did not. Time may be either infinite or finite. Apart from religious faith, we will never be able to know whether the cosmos—and, with it, time and motion—is or is not everlasting in its existence.

While Aquinas, the philosopher, insists upon retaining a completely open mind on the question, Aquinas, the man of faith and sacred theologian, answers both questions—the question about the world's having an end as well as the question about the world's having a beginning. It will certainly not surprise the reader to learn that Aquinas, in line with the creed of his religion, affirmed that the world began when it was created by God. However, it may surprise the reader to learn that, in Question 104 in Part One of the *Summa Theologica*, Aquinas also declared that God annihilates nothing. The cosmos, exnihilated by God at its beginning, is not brought to an end by a Divine act of annihilation. This is more fully explained in the concluding treatise of the *Summa*, which deals with "last things"—the transformation of the world after its final conflagration.

The position taken by Aquinas the philosopher was adopted many centuries later by the German philosopher, Immanuel Kant. In that section of his *Critique of Pure Reason* which sets forth what he calls "the cosmological antinomies," Kant argues, as Aquinas argued earlier, that the question whether time is infinite or finite and the question whether the world has a beginning and end cannot be decided by reason. These are matters beyond the power of reason to determine.

Where does all this leave us? A pagan approach to the question of God's existence must certainly eschew the position taken by persons of religious faith. To affirm, with them, that the world or cosmos had an absolute beginning—that it was exnihilated at an initial instant—would be tantamount to affirming the existence of God, the world's exnihilator. We must, in short, avoid the error of begging the question—the error of assuming the truth of the proposition to be proved or argued for.

Science is silent and may always remain silent on the question. The rejection of the steady state hypothesis and the adoption of the big bang hypothesis allow us a free choice between the assumption that the cosmos had an absolute beginning and the assumption that it has always existed. Philosophy—in the persons of Aquinas and Kant—insists that neither of these alternative assumptions is more tenable than the other.

To assume that the cosmos had an absolute beginning—that it was exnihilated at some initial instant—has exactly the same effect as to accept the dogmatic assertion made by persons of religious faith. It begs the question. It assumes that God, the exnihilator, exists.

A purely philosophical and pagan approach to the problem of proving God's existence, or at least of attempting to discover grounds for regarding belief in God to be eminently reasonable, must, therefore, steadfastly and stringently avoid the error mentioned—the error of begging the question by assuming what is to be proved. To do this, we must proceed on the assumption of an everlasting cosmos, the assumption that the universe has always existed and will always continue in existence—everlasting in an infinite time, time without beginning or end.

As we proceed to engage in purely philosophical and pagan thinking about God, we must resolutely exclude from our minds the notion or imagery of an initial act of creation or exnihilation. We must do more than that. We must also exclude from our minds the notion that the things of this world, including ourselves, are "creatures."

That word is frequently used in contemporary speech by irreligious persons who seem unaware of its implication. Those who do not believe in God, the creator, should not refer to anything as a creature. Likewise, a purely philosophical and pagan inquiry into the question of God's existence, proceeding without any light or direction drawn from religious faith, should have no commerce with the notion that the things around us and ourselves are not only parts or components of the natural world, but also creatures of God.

CHAPTER 5

No First Cause

ANOTHER ERROR TO BE AVOIDED is the traditionally persistent and widely prevalent notion that an inquiry concerning God's existence is an inquiry concerning the existence of a first cause. This is not to say that we must reject the notion of cause entirely. On the contrary, among the ways of arguing for God's existence, any mode of argument that starts from the things of this world as we know them, or from the world as a whole, will be an argument that involves reference to causation. To exclude the notion of a first cause as illegitimate is, therefore, not to exclude the notion of cause as such.

It may not be possible to construct a chain of reasoning that leads to the conclusion "Therefore, God exists" without including a step that refers to God as the cause of some known effect—an effect that cannot be causally explained without positing the existence of God as its cause. It is not only quite possible (as I will endeavor to show), it is also quite necessary to formulate such reasoning without placing God as the first member in a series of causes, the last of which produces the effect that is to be explained.

A series of causes and effects is a series occurring in time. Let Z stand for the effect to be explained. Let Y stand for its proximate cause. But unless Y is itself an uncaused cause, it is itself an effect that requires a cause. Let that cause be X. What is true of Y is also true of X, and so on backward in a chain of temporally successive causes and effects.

Is that chain finite or infinite in extent? Does it begin with some first cause in the series, a cause that is not an effect and so has no prior cause? Or does it have no beginning, every link in the chain, backward from the effect with which we started, being itself an effect of some prior cause?

To say that there must be some first cause—some uncaused cause in the series of causes and effects—is to assume that time is finite and that change, together with its causation, began with the operation of that first cause. This is the same as saying that the cosmos had a beginning. As we have seen, we must avoid that assumption because it begs the question.

The opposite assumption, which we found it necessary to adopt, is not repugnant to reason. It is not repugnant to reason to assume that the cosmos always existed, that there is no beginning to change or causation, that time is infinite, and that there is an infinite series of causes and effects. In such a series, there can be no first cause.

Those who have been brought up in the firmly established traditions of Western theology, both sacred and natural, will be quick to reply that what is meant by "first cause" is not "first in a temporal series of causes and effects," but rather "first, or highest, in a simultaneously cooperative set of causes."

To get a picture of what is meant by this, consider the

causes operative in the painting of a picture. The brush that touches the canvas and applies the pigments is one cause; the hand of the painter, another; and the mind of the painter, a third. The mind of the painter moves the hand that holds the brush and the hand moves the brush as it touches the canvas. The effect—the painting—is thus produced. In the production of that effect, the three causes operate simultaneously: the motion of the painter's hand is caused by the action of his mind; the motion of the painter's brush is caused by the motion of his hand. In this set of simultaneously cooperating causes, the painter's mind is the first or principal cause; his hand, a secondary instrumental cause, and his brush, a tertiary instrumental cause.

Since we are well acquainted with the phenomena of artistic production, and since we understand the causal relation of the action of the painter's mind to the motion of his hand and the causal relation of the motion of his hand to the motion of his brush, we have no difficulty in arranging these three causes in a hierarchical set, in which the painter's mind is the first or principal cause and the remaining causes are all instrumental—secondary and tertiary.

However, when we pass from artistic production to the phenomena of nature, we do not find anything comparable to a set of simultaneously cooperative causes which can be hierarchically arranged. All natural causes seem to be on the same level or of the same grade. Though it may frequently be the case that a natural effect is produced by the cooperation of a set of causes, none of these stands to the others as a principal cause stands to an instrumental cause.

We must, of course, pay attention to what the traditional theologian had in mind when he asked us to interpret "first" as *highest* in a set of simultaneously cooperative causes, not as number one in a temporally successive series of causes. According to our theologian, all the natural causes simultaneously involved in the production of any natural effect are together secondary and instrumental causes. The theologian will then tell us that such causes, being only instrumental, cannot function unless they are brought into operation by a principal cause—a first cause only in the sense that it is at the top of a hierarchically ordered, finite set of causes.

Two things should be noted about this argument. First, it maintains that an infinite ascent upward in such a hierarchically ordered set of causes is unacceptable, as an infinite regression backward in a temporally successive series of causes is not. It is repugnant to reason because, in such a set of causes, if there were no first cause that moved the secondary instrumental causes to action, none of the secondary instrumental causes would operate to produce the effect that is to be explained. Wherever there are instrumental causes, there must be a principal cause, and that principal cause is entitled to be called a first cause in relation to all the secondary causes that are instrumental in relation to it.

Second, the argument does not need to picture the set of causes as consisting in more than two levels of causation. It does not need to regard the instrumental causes as hierarchically ordered, one secondary, another tertiary, and so on. It suffices for the purposes of the argument if all the natural causes simultaneously cooperative in the production of a natural effect are on the same level—all secondary causes, all instrumental causes. When they are so regarded, they all stand in the same relation to the one principal or first cause, without whose action their own action does not take place.

The trouble with the argument as so clarified and refined is that we have no reason whatsoever for regarding natural causes as secondary or instrumental. To so regard them is tantamount to saying that the consideration of their action does not suffice to explain the natural effects we observe. That, in turn, amounts to saying that natural science cannot

possibly give an adequate account of natural phenomena—
that any causal explanation which refers only to natural
causes must fail to do what it certainly appears to do.

In the case of the painter and the painting, we start out
knowing the relation of the causes involved in the production of the work of art. But in the case of natural phenomena,
we start out knowing only how the phenomena we study
are related, and from that we come to see which is cause and
which is effect. Nothing requires us to go behind the scene
to find a hidden principal cause that is pulling the strings
to make these natural puppets move. Nothing requires us to
rise above the plane on which all natural causes operate to
the level of a supernatural cause that moves all these natural
causes, whether they are arranged in series or in sets.

We can never infer the existence of an unobserved and
unobservable principal cause. Unless we already know that it
exists, we have no ground for regarding other observed
causes as serving it in an instrumental fashion.

What the sacred theologian affirms may still be true. It
may still be true that God cooperates in the occurrence of
everything that happens in nature, as a principal cause cooperates with instrumental causes. But we have no basis for
inferring that that is the case from our study and understanding of the operation of natural causes. Our understanding of their operation quite suffices to explain everything in
the realm of natural phenomena that needs to be explained.

I do not mean by this that science is perfect and that we
have already achieved a complete explanation of natural
phenomena. But, in order to improve upon the explanations
we are now able to give, we need only to pursue our scientific inquiries further and acquire more knowledge of nature
and a better understanding of it. We do not need to sup-
plement science with theology; we do not need to refer to
a first or principal cause in order to remedy the deficiency
of natural causes as explanatory of natural effects.

So far, we have been considering only motions and changes, and the causes thereof. All the causes with which we are acquainted in the physical world (the world of natural phenomena) are causes of this kind—causes of change or motion. But existence—the existence of individual things or of the whole congeries of such things that is the world as a whole—may also require a causal explanation. If it does, then natural causes may not suffice, for natural causes appear to be solely causes of change or motion, not of existence.

A biological progenitor, for example, only causes a change —the becoming or coming into existence of the progeny. It does not cause the continuing existence of the offspring after its procreation. Whether that needs to be explained by causes, and, if it does, how such causation operates, remain to be seen.

For the present, the only point I wish to make concerns a serious error, prevalent in traditional theology, which should be avoided in a purely philosophical inquiry concerning God's existence.

The error is present in any attempt to reason to God's existence either by working back to God as the indispensable first or initial cause in a temporally ordered series of successive causes, or by working up to God as the indispensable first or principal cause in a hierarchically arranged set of simultaneous causes.

From such knowledge as we have of the things of this world, or from our knowledge of the cosmos as a whole, we have no grounds for affirming God's existence because we think that the operation of a first cause—either a first initial or a first principal cause—is necessary to explain whatever phenomena need explanation.

Let me repeat once more the reason why such inferences are illegitimate. The fact that we are compelled to assume an infinite extension of time from the present backward, as inseparable from our assumption that the cosmos has always existed, precludes us from rejecting an infinite temporal series of causes and effects. Consistent with the position he took in his dispute with the Averroists about the eternity of the world, Aquinas flatly declared that he found nothing repugnant to reason in an infinite series of parents and children, or of progenitors and progeny. So much for no inference to God as the first, initial cause in a temporally ordered series of causes and effects.

With regard to a hierarchically ordered set of simultaneously cooperative causes, we can never say which one is the first or principal cause and which are the secondary or instrumental causes unless we are directly acquainted with all these causes in their cooperative functioning, as, indeed, we are in the case of a painter producing a painting. The existence and operation of a hidden or unobservable principal cause cannot be inferred from the operation of observable natural causes that are thoroughly efficacious in the production of their effects.

There is no reason to regard the observable natural causes as merely instrumental and as, therefore, needing a principal cause to make them efficacious. Hence there is no ground for inferring God's existence and operation as the first, principal cause in a hierarchically arranged set of causes.

If we avoid the error of trying to argue for the existence of God on the ground that God is needed as a first cause, a closely connected error will also be avoided. That is the mistake of thinking that the motions and changes which occur in nature cannot be explained without positing God as their cause. As we have seen, that is not the case. So far as reason can tell, the non-existence of God would leave the phenomena of nature unaffected. Both what happens and the explanation of what happens in the world would remain the same—on the supposition, of course, that the world can exist without God.

PART THREE

Setting the Stage

CHAPTER 6

The Uniqueness of the Word 'God'

IN THE PRECEDING PAGES, the word "God" has been used again and again, and used without explanation of its meaning.

What went through your mind, I would like to ask the reader, when you read sentences containing the word? Were you stopped by it because it was as meaningless to you as a word in a foreign language, or as a word not in your vocabulary?

The answer to this question will, I am sure, be different for different readers. Those who are persons of religious faith will, of course, attach to the word the meaning that is determined for them by the doctrine that underlies their religious beliefs. That meaning will be more or less clear and precise, depending on the degree to which they understand the doctrine involved.

Pagan readers may attach to the word some of the connotations they have learned from their acquaintance with religious doctrines in which they do not themselves believe. Quite apart from that, the word will not be a stranger to the vocabulary of most, if not all, readers of this book. It will have some meaning for those who claim to have no interest in the question whether God exists, for those who call themselves atheists and deny that God exists, as well as for those who, while not believing in God, are at least interested and willing to inquire into the question of God's existence.

The meaning of the word is not likely to be the same for all. Yet there is, perhaps, some thread of meaning common to the diverse connotations attached to the word by all who use it, enough to prevent the word from being completely equivocal, as the word "rest" is equivocal when it is used in physics to name the opposite of motion, on the one hand, and a residue or remainder, on the other hand.

If that were not the case, then the atheist who denies God's existence, the agnostic who thinks that he cannot discover anything about God by rational inquiry, and the theist who affirms God's existence, either by faith or by reason, would not be opposed to one another and would have nothing to argue about.

Even the pantheist, who identifies God with the infinite cosmos, thereby annulling the distinction between the natural and the supernatural, retains some meaning for the word "God" that preserves what the word names as an object of reverence, if not of worship. It is necessary to add at once that the pantheist's use of the word would appear to foreclose any inquiry about whether God exists. It may even be contended that the word as used by the pantheist verges on equivocation or crosses the line.

Acceptance of the state of affairs described above will not do for the purposes of this inquiry. Everyone concerned with the question whether X exists must attach the same meaning to the word that names or designates X; and that meaning must be made as clear and precise as possible. Scientific inquiries, in which the X in question may be a certain kind of elementary particle or a certain celestial body, would not proceed without first giving as much clarity and precision as possible to the word that is used to name or designate X.

The same cannot be said for theological inquiries concerning God's existence as they have been traditionally carried on, probably because they have been carried on for the most part by men of religious faith who were content to adopt the meaning for the word "God" derived from the doctrine of their faith.

In this purely philosophical and pagan inquiry concerning God's existence, we must proceed in a manner much more closely akin to scientific inquiry. Not only must we refrain from relying on any of the connotations attached to the word "God" by the religious doctrines of the West; we must go further and try to shut those connotations out of our mind as we attempt to discover what meaning we find ourselves obliged to assign the word, on the basis of rational considerations alone.

However, before that, we must first pay attention to the word itself. It is a noun and, like other nouns, it is a name word designating an object that either exists or about which we can ask whether or not it does exist. Among nouns that are name words, some designate singular or unique objects and some refer to classes of objects, members of which either exist or about which we can ask whether or not they exist.

For example, the word "horse" refers to a class of animals that zoologists can define with some precision. Our perceptual experience leaves us with no doubt that horses exist— that the class of animals defined is not empty or without members. The word "centaur" or "mermaid" also refers to a class of organisms that mythology has defined with some precision, but here we also have little or no doubt that no centaurs or mermaids exist. We have never met with any instances of the class, instances in which existence is a matter of perceptual experience.

To take one further example, "angel" also names a class of objects, in this case a class defined by sacred theology. Those who believe in angels will affirm, and those who do not believe in angels will deny, that angels exist, but they can only join issue on this question if both attach the same meaning to the word "angel"—the meaning given that word by theologians who define the class of objects in question.

So far, all the examples considered are nouns or name words that signify classes of objects, objects of thought which may or may not have perceptible instances. All such nouns or name words are called "common nouns" or "common names," precisely because they signify a group of objects that belong to a class the members of which have certain characteristics in common.

Among common nouns, some are regarded as "concrete" and some as "abstract"—concrete, when perceptible instances of the class can be found or looked for; abstract when the class is of such a character that the objects in question are intrinsically imperceptible, and therefore are exclusively objects of thought, never perceptual objects. "Horse" and "centaur" are concrete class names; "justice" and "infinity" abstract ones. Even though a common noun or class name is abstract, it remains possible to ask whether or not the class has members, whether or not instances of the class exist, instances which may not be perceptible but concerning the existence of which evidence may be marshaled or reasons advanced.

Now let us turn to that large group of nouns or name words which designate singular or unique objects—one and only one. They are ordinarily distinguished from common nouns or names by being called "proper nouns" or "proper names." The object they designate may have something in common with other objects. The singular or unique object named may be a member of this or that class of objects. In other words, the object named may not only be a singular individual, but also a particular instance of a class of objects.

The author of this book is a particular instance of the class named by the word "man," the class named by the word "philosopher," the class named by the word "pagan." But his name "Mortimer J. Adler" does not tell you that. You have to learn that by reading this book or a brief biographical note. All that "Mortimer J. Adler" tells you by the way it is written is that, being a proper name, it refers to a singular individual. In order for you to be able to use this proper name, that singular individual has to be identified for you, either through direct acquaintance—by your being introduced to the object named or by having the object named pointed out to you—or through a definite description of the object named, such as the one given on the jacket of this book.

About half of the article titles in the *Encyclopaedia Britannica* are proper names—the names of singular persons or places, singular institutions, objects, or events. No one has any difficulty in recognizing which article titles in *Encyclopaedia Britannica* are proper names and which are common: the former have their initial letters capitalized, the latter do not.

Modern mathematical logic, for reasons peculiar to itself, has raised a host of difficulties about proper names, even to the point of denying that there are or can be any. But in our daily life, as persons of common sense and common experience, we have little or no difficulty in knowing whether the word we are using names a singular object or a class of objects. If we did have such difficulty, we would not know, as we most certainly do, when it is or is not correct to capitalize the initial letter of the noun we are writing.

By dismissing the special concerns of mathematical logic as having little interest for us, I am not overlooking the fact that proper names do present certain difficulties of which we should be aware. For example, the proper name "Thomas Aquinas" has been used in the preceding pages, and readers of this book, who may not have heard of him before, have become acquainted with the singular person named by what I have said about him. They know that he was a Roman Catholic theologian, living in the 13th century, who wrote many books, among which are the *Summa Theologica* and the *Summa Contra Gentiles*. They also know that he was a disciple of Aristotle and that he disputed certain matters with followers of Averroës at the University of Paris. These facts about him are quite sufficient to identify for them the singular object named, even though he cannot become for them an object of direct acquaintance, a person to whom they can be introduced or one who can be pointed out to them.

The singularity of the Thomas Aquinas referred to above does not preclude the use of "Thomas Aquinas" as a proper name for some other singular object. I have, for example, a Burmese cat to which my family has given the name "Thomas Aquinas." When he is not visibly present and I use that name to call him to me, I know that I am not summoning a mediaeval theologian to reappear on earth. I have no difficulty about using "Thomas Aquinas" as a proper name for two quite different singular individuals—one a mediaeval theologian and the other a living cat—because, in each case, I have in mind a quite different definite description of the object named.

Nor should readers of this book have any difficulty about it. Henceforward, they can use the proper name "Thomas Aquinas" for two quite distinct singular objects, though they have no direct acquaintance with either. In one case, they can use the proper name for a person that has been sufficiently identified in the course of the preceding pages; in the other case, they can use it for a cat that has now been identified as the pet of Mortimer Adler, the author of this book.

If others who are not readers of this book hear the proper name "Mortimer J. Adler" for the first time, or see it in writing, the only thing they know at first is that they are confronted with a proper name, but they do not yet know the singular object named. If they go to the Chicago telephone book, they may discover a number of instances of that same proper name. They will still not be able to use it, as it should be used, to designate one and only one individual. They cannot use it as proper names are intended to be used until one of three things happens: (1) someone introduces them to a perceived individual who is called by that proper name; (2) someone points out a perceived individual, called by that proper name; or (3) they are given a definite description of the object named, a description that is sufficient to identify a unique individual, the same individual denoted by that proper name. Two or more individuals may have the same proper name (for example, "Thomas Aquinas"), but a given definite description will be applicable to one and one only.

One more example may drive home this important point about proper names and definite descriptions. As I am writing this book, the one and only president of the United States is Jimmy Carter. If someone hears the proper name "Jimmy Carter" for the first time, and, not being introduced to the singular individual named or not having that individual pointed out to him, asks who Jimmy Carter is, the answer "president of the United States of America in the year 1980" should suffice as a definite description to identify the singular object that I have in mind when I use "Jimmy Carter" as a proper name.

All this is preparation for our consideration of the unique

character of the word "God." It is clearly intended to be used as a proper name. As so used, it should designate a singular object. But it differs from all other proper names in a number of important respects that make it unique among proper names and among all other words in our vocabulary.

In the case of every other proper name, the singular object named, while unique and therefore deserving of a proper name, is also an object of a certain kind and belongs to one or more classes of objects that can be defined. Thomas Aquinas, the mediaeval theologian, is a philosopher and a human being; Thomas Aquinas, our household pet, is a male Burmese cat.

Like every other proper name, "God" designates a unique object, but one which does not belong to any class of objects. "Zeus" and "Apollo" are proper names that designate unique objects, but they are also objects that belong to the class known as the gods worshiped by the ancient Greeks, a class that includes Aphrodite and Pallas Athena as well.

When we use "God" as a proper name in this inquiry, we are using it to designate an object that is not only unique, as every other singular individual is, but one that is also unclassifiable.

Not all proper names designate singular individuals the existence of which is either known or taken for granted. The telephone book is full of proper names that designate singular individuals, the existence of which you take for granted even though you may be unacquainted with most of the persons named. This is also true of most of the persons named in historical narratives. When you take the existence of the individual named for granted, you are assuming that the individual in question could have been introduced or pointed out to someone else, even if circumstances prevent you from being directly acquainted with that person. That is true of Alexander the Great, Julius Caesar, Napoleon, and Wellington.

What about "Hamlet" as a proper name? It designates a

singular individual who is a character in Shakespeare's play of that title, who is an object of imagination but never a perceptual object for anyone, and so is a unique person who is imaginary rather than real. Here, then, is a proper name that designates a singular object which we know did not, does not, and will not exist in reality.

What about "Raphael" and "Gabriel" as proper names of two archangels mentioned in the Old Testament? For those of religious faith who believe in the reality of angels, these proper names designate really existent objects. For others, they designate objects that are as purely imaginary as Shakespeare's Hamlet.

It is, therefore, possible for a word to be used as a proper name even though the unique individual it designates may be one the real existence of which can be questioned and disputed. "God" is a proper name of this sort.

If we exclude all the proper names that we use for objects known by us to be imaginary and not real, then all the proper names that remain are those we can use to designate objects the reality of which we (1) know by direct acquaintance, (2) take for granted, or (3) question.

In this inquiry, "God" names a singular object the real existence of which is in question. In that respect, the word "God," as a proper name, is like "Raphael" and "Gabriel"—archangels the existence of which is affirmed by some and denied by others. Those who affirm the existence of Raphael and Gabriel do so on the basis of their faith in the Old Testament as the revealed word of God and on their believing what they have read about Raphael in the *Book of Tobit* or about Gabriel in the *Book of Daniel*.

What is true of "Raphael" and "Gabriel" as proper names is not true of "God." Even those who believe in the existence of God do not use "God" as a proper name for an object with whom any human being on earth can be directly acquainted, through introduction or pointing.

The word "God" is thus seen to be unique among proper

names. As in the case of certain other proper names, it designates an object the real existence of which is questionable, and which is affirmed by some and denied by others. But in the case of "God" the question of the real existence of the object named, or the issue between those who affirm and those who deny the real existence of that object, cannot be resolved by direct acquaintance on our part or by an appeal to the testimony of those who report having had such direct acquaintance with the object named.

Against what I have just said, it may be contended, first, that direct acquaintance with God in the person of Jesus Christ was vouchsafed to his disciples and others with whom he had contact on earth. Similarly, it may be said that Abraham, to whom God spoke in the wilderness, or Moses, who heard God's voice on Mount Sinai, had personal acquaintance with God. However, in both cases, as in the case of the archangels, religious faith is prerequisite to acknowledging such acquaintance. There were many who lived in the presence of Jesus Christ who did not have the faith that would make them acknowledge their personal acquaintance with God. Pagans certainly, whether pagans in antiquity or pagans alive today, would not hesitate to deny that personal acquaintance with God is out of the question.

Second, it may be contended that the proper name of a real as opposed to an imaginary individual should *always* designate an object the real existence of which can be established by direct acquaintance on the part of someone. If the object named really exists, it should be possible to introduce it to someone, either in the past, present, or future, not just describe it in words that identify it, as Shakespeare's Hamlet can be described, or as Zeus and Gabriel can be described. Even if the object named by the word "God" really exists, it lies totally beyond the reach of direct acquaintance— beyond introduction or pointing out, and, therefore, "God" is not, strictly speaking, a proper name.

Granting the merit of what has been said, we are led to the conclusion that "God" is like all other proper names in that it is a word devised to designate a unique or singular object. It is like some proper names in that it is a word devised to designate an object the real existence of which is questioned and disputed. But "God" is different from the aforementioned proper names in that the issue about the real existence of the object named cannot be resolved either by direct acquaintance or by appeal to the testimony of those who claim to have had direct acquaintance with it.

The further consequence this conclusion carries is that we must be prepared to substitute for the word "God," used as a proper name, a definite description of the object named. In lieu of any possibility of direct acquaintance with the object named, so far as pagans are concerned, a definite description must be formulated to identify the object the real existence of which is in question.

In the case of "Julius Caesar" or "Napoleon," those of us alive today must also be satisfied with definite descriptions to identify the objects named, since we cannot have direct acquaintance with them. In these cases, we can also consider the testimony of individuals living in the past who had direct acquaintance with them. But when, as pagans, we use the word "God" as a proper name, our only handle on the word must be a definite description that designates the singular, unique, and unclassifiable object that we have in mind when we ask whether or not God exists.

CHAPTER 7

Why We Must Substitute a Definite Description for "God"

A DEFINITE DESCRIPTION DESIGNATES a unique, singular object, not a class of objects. It is so called because it is like a proper name that we apply to an individual we know. The phrase "presidents of the United States" is not a definite description because it designates a class having two or more members; but "the president of the United States in June 1980" is a definite description because it identifies one and only one individual.

Though definite, it is not a definition. Unique, singular objects—individuals—cannot be defined. The classification of the physical elements, or the classification of plants and animals, requires scientists to define the classes that they differentiate and order in relation to one another. But individual members of these classes cannot be defined; they can only be identified. Such identification, as we have seen, must sometimes be accomplished by a definite description, and it is successfully accomplished only if the definite description is detailed enough to be applicable to one and only one individual.

In discussions of God, one is likely to ask: "How do you define God?" One should know, of course, that God, like any other unique, singular object, cannot be defined. One should ask: "What is the character of the object you have in mind when you use the word 'God'?" Or: "What are you referring to when you use the word 'God'?" A proper answer to such questions can be given only in the form of a definite description which identifies the object in question, so that the persons engaged in the conversation are able to talk about one and the same object.

Any other unique, singular object that we try to identify by a definite description is classifiable in a large number of different ways. It is a member of many different classes. This enables us to refer to one or more of these classes in constructing a definite description of the individual in question. For example, in the case of Thomas Aquinas, we can refer to his being a Roman Catholic, a disciple of Aristotle, a theologian, and a teacher at the University of Paris; but he is also that one among Roman Catholics, disciples of Aristotle, theologians, teachers at the University of Paris, who was born in the year 1225, died in the year 1274, and wrote the *Summa Contra Gentiles* in the years 1256–1259.

Of all the unique, singular objects that we may try to identify by definite descriptions, only God is unclassifiable. In constructing a definite description of God, we cannot use words that signify classes to which other objects belong; or, if that kind of word does creep into our definite description of God, we must be very wary of it and closely examine the sense in which it is said of God, as distinct from the sense in which it is said of other objects. Constructing a definite description of God is, therefore, a task of extraordinary difficulty.

We shall presently attempt to compare God with other objects of thought. We may discover that God is like other objects of thought in a certain respect. If that turns out to be the case, the statement just made—that God is unclassifiable—may be challenged because we normally suppose that what is unclassifiable must also be incomparable with anything else.

If one thing is like others in a certain respect, they can all be said to belong to the same class, for a class consists of individuals that are all alike in a given respect. How, then, can God be like other objects of thought in any respect and still be unclassifiable?

The answer is as follows. When two or more things are said to belong to the same class *because they are alike in a certain respect*, the word that names the respect in which they are alike must be applied to them *in exactly the same sense*. But, as we shall presently see, no name can ever be applied to God and any other object in exactly the same sense.

When we bear in mind this important point about the diversity of meaning that is inescapable in the use of any given word to characterize God and other objects, we realize that it is not inconsistent to say that God is unclassifiable and also to say that God is like other objects of thought in a certain respect.

One further objection may still be raised. Does not the reference to God as an object of thought put God in the same class with all other objects of thought? It must be conceded that the phrase "object of thought"—as applied to God and other objects of thought—is used in exactly the same sense.

What, now, is the reason for persisting in the view that God is unclassifiable? Here a different answer explains the reason why.

A class of objects must not only include as its members

all entities that possess whatever characteristic defines the class; it must also exclude from membership all entities that do not possess that characteristic. Nothing that is thinkable is excluded from the class signified by the phrase "object of thought." Everything we can think of—God and everything else—is an object of thought.

The phrase "object of thought" does not, therefore, define a genuine class. For this reason it remains correct to say that God, while an object of thought, is unclassifiable.

When we construct a definite description of God, we are saying, first of all, that the definite description we have formulated is equivalent to or substitutable for the word "God" as a proper name: It designates one and the same unique, singular object. We are doing more than that. The word "God" by itself (without having a definite description attached to it) has no connotative significance. That is why persons engaged in a conversation about God are likely to ask what the word means. They may make the mistake of thinking they are asking for a definition of God. They would be equally mistaken if they thought they were seeking a conception of God.

It is of the utmost importance to explain the latter mistake. Readers may have no difficulty in understanding why they should not ask for a definition of God, but they may wonder why they should not ask the person who uses the word "God" to state his or her conception of God.

The explanation requires us to pay attention to certain differences among the objects with which we have acquaintance through sense experience. In the world of physical objects, some, like horses, mushrooms, and diamonds, are objects of perceptual experience. We perceive them immediately and directly by means of our senses without the aid of any instruments of observation. Another group of objects are perceptible by us only when the acuity of our senses is magnified by such instruments of observation as telescopes and microscopes. With their assistance, we can perceive the structure of cells or distant heavenly bodies beyond the range of ordinary vision.

Another class of objects is not directly or immediately perceptible. In this case, what we perceive are the traces such objects leave or the effects they produce on our experimental screens or registers. They are thus detectable in the same way that a distant forest fire is detected by our perception of a column of smoke rising in the sky. We are not perceiving the fire; we are detecting it, and inferring its existence from our perception of an effect it is producing.

Nuclear particles of all sorts are physical objects of this kind, not only electrons and protons, but also baryons, mesons, neutrinos, and quarks. The same can be said of such astronomical objects as black holes, or even the cosmos itself. We come to know physical objects of this kind in an indirect fashion by detection and inference, by the interpretation of experimental observations or of perceived pointer readings on scientific instruments.

Nuclear physicists with whom I have discussed the matter are agreed that the elementary particles investigated in subatomic or nuclear physics are radically different from perceptible physical objects of the first two kinds—those we are able to perceive directly, one kind by our unaided senses and the other by means of such instruments of observation as telescopes and microscopes. Nevertheless, since elementary particles are physical objects, they are detectable by laboratory observations, even though they are not, strictly speaking, themselves perceptible.

I hope to show presently that we cannot think of God as a physical object. Consequently, we must think of God not only as inherently imperceptible, but also as inherently undetectable in the way that elementary particles or black holes are detectable. Of course, persons of religious faith may claim that some physical incarnation or manifestation of

God has been vouchsafed to certain human beings on earth; but pagans, lacking such faith, will reject that claim and insist that God, not being a physical object, is not perceptible or empirically detectable.

We cannot form an empirical concept of any object that is not directly and immediately perceived by us, as horses, mushrooms, and diamonds are, as well as microscopically observed cells or telescopically observed distant stars. The reason is simply that empirical concepts are concepts formed on the basis of our sense perception of observable and observed objects.

Such words as "horse," "mushroom," and "diamond" express empirical concepts, but such words as "electron," "proton," "baryon," "meson," or "black hole" and "cosmos" do not. Many of the technical terms in contemporary physical science are of the latter sort, as are many terms in psychology as well, terms such as "unconscious" or even the term "mental state."

However, such terms do express some notion or understanding on our part. That notion or understanding is based on empirical evidence of one sort or another. But the notion or understanding we have is not directly derived from our experience of the object in question, whereas in the case of horses, mushrooms, and diamonds, it is.

Using the term "empirical concept" for the notions or understandings that we derive directly from our acquaintance with objects of thought that are also objects of immediate perceptual experience, we must use some other term for our notions about objects of thought that are not also objects of immediate perceptual experience.

Logicians, studying the methods and content of modern science, have improvised the term we are seeking. They have distinguished between empirical concepts, on the one hand, and theoretical constructs, on the other hand, the latter consisting in the notions or understandings we have of objects of thought that are not objects of immediate perceptual experience.

The technical scientific terms that I have already mentioned as words that do not express empirical concepts (for example, "electron" or "baryon" in nuclear physics, "black hole" in astronomy, "unconscious" in psychology) are the kinds of words that express theoretical constructs. The word "God" belongs with them rather than with such words as "horse," "mushroom," and "diamond" which do express empirical concepts. When we think of God, as when we think of electrons or black holes, we do so by means of a theoretical construct, not by means of an empirical concept.

However, there are two important differences between God, on the one hand, and the physical objects that we must employ theoretical constructs to think of. Physical objects, as we have noted, are either perceptible or empirically detectable. God, not being a physical object, is neither.

The other important difference between our notion of God and our notion of electrons or black holes lies in the fact that we can state our notion of electrons or black holes in the form of something like a definition that describes a whole class of objects, not just a unique, singular object. By means of our theoretically constructed notion of electrons or black holes, we can understand all the electrons or black holes that may exist, not just one.

Our notion of God cannot be stated in the form of a definition. Rather, it must be stated in the form of a definite description of God. When we thereby express our notion of God, that notion, like the notion of an electron or a black hole, is a theoretical construct, not an empirical concept.

The reader may quite justifiably wonder why I have thought it necessary to be so insistent about the distinction between empirical concepts and theoretical constructs. One answer is that logical clarity and precision require it. However, that is not the only answer, or the most important one.

The reader should see at once that, if modern scientists can legitimately and validly deal with objects that lie wholly outside the range of ordinary or common experience because they cannot be directly perceived by us, and are able to do so by means of notions that are theoretical constructs rather than empirical concepts, then theologians cannot be dismissed as being engaged in illegitimate and invalid speculation when they also deal with objects that lie outside the range of ordinary or common experience, and also do so by means of notions that are theoretical constructs rather than empirical concepts.

Theological inquiry employs such notions, not only the notion of God, but also the notion of the cosmos as a whole. As we shall see, theological inquiry involves other notions that are theoretical constructs. The notional apparatus of theology, like that of nuclear physics and 20th-century cosmology, consists mainly of theoretical constructs.

I have one further reason for stressing the point under consideration. The great German philosopher Immanuel Kant, who wrote his *Critique of Pure Reason* toward the end of the 18th century, has been called "the thunderer." One clap of his thunder was directed against what he took to be traditional theological speculation, especially the attempt to establish the existence of God by reason and reason alone.

His thundering issued from a theory of knowledge which was critical of any attempt on the part of reason to deal with objects that lie beyond the range of experience. To do so, he maintained, was an illegitimate and illusory use of reason. The empirical concepts that he thought reason must employ cannot be validly employed in thinking about non-empirical objects, the most eminently non-empirical object being God.

Kant's theory of knowledge should have been discredited in the eyes of the world by the non-Euclidean geometries and the post-Newtonian physics with which he was unacquainted. That his theory of knowledge is still respected in certain quarters is quite remarkable.

Be that as it may, his strictures against theological inquiry lose all their force when we recognize that theology, like nuclear physics and cosmology in the 20th century, uses theoretical constructs, not empirical concepts, to deal with objects that lie beyond the range of ordinary or common experience. If, for that reason, theological inquiry cannot be legitimately and validly conducted, the same reason would make nuclear physics and contemporary cosmology illegitimate and invalid enterprises.

CHAPTER 8

How to Formulate a Definite Description of God: First Step

Lᴇᴛ ᴍᴇ ʙᴇɢɪɴ by reminding the reader of the central point to be learned from the preceding chapter. When we have succeeded in formulating a definite description of God, we will have achieved a notion of God that is a theoretical construct, not an empirical concept.

How is this to be accomplished? Until very recently, I thought that a famous argument, called the "ontological argument," provided the means for doing so. That argument was the brilliant invention of Anselm, an archbishop of Canterbury in the 11th century. It is often mistakenly interpreted as a valid argument for God's existence—even by certain 20th-century philosophers, some of whom may be pagans.

Reserving for Chapter 11 my reasons for thinking this to be an erroneous interpretation of the ontological argument,

I wish here only to indicate how Anselm helps us to take at least a first step toward formulating a definite description of God.

Being a man of profound religious faith, Anselm sought to reach an understanding or notion of God that would support his faith and, perhaps, also explicate it. He prefaced his effort by saying that he longed to understand the truth in which his heart believed, adding that he did not seek to understand in order to believe, but rather that he believed in order to understand, for unless he believed, he would not understand.

The argument then begins with the statement of his religious belief, a belief shared by Jews and Muslims as well as Christians. We believe, Anselm declares, that God is a being than which no greater can be thought of. In rendering the foregoing statement, I have substituted "a being than which no greater can be *thought of*" for the usual rendition—"a being than which no greater can be *conceived*"—in order to remain consistent with the point made in the preceding chapter that, strictly speaking, we may have a notion, but no conception, of God.

A theoretical construct that is a complex notion will involve a number of distinct, though related, notes. The note expressed by the words "a being than which no greater can be thought of" can also be expressed by the words "supreme being." Since there cannot be two supreme beings, we should not think of God as *a* supreme being, but rather as *the* supreme being—the one and only being than which no greater can be thought of.

So far we have interpreted Anselm's argument as introducing only one note—that of supremacy. A second and third are introduced by what follows.

Anselm points out that even a person who does not believe in God's existence can understand what is meant by the words "a being than which no greater can be thought of." He can hold before his mind the notion of such a being, even though he does not believe or think that such a being exists in reality—outside his mind or apart from his thinking of it.

Anselm then calls our attention to the fact that for an object to be solely an object of thought is not the same as its being something that really exists outside our mind and apart from our thinking of it, in addition to being an object that is before our minds when we do think of it.

This point he illustrates by referring to the painter who first has some notion or understanding of what he is going to produce on the canvas. Until he produces it, the painter knows that the picture he is thinking of exists solely in his mind. Only after he has produced it, will it exist in reality as well.

The final step in the argument follows immediately. Let us suppose that those who have a notion of the supreme being (a being than which no greater can be thought of) think that the supreme being exists only in their minds as an object of thought, but does not also exist in reality, as the painting exists after the painter has produced it. Cannot someone else say to them that they have made a mistake in thinking this? For if the supreme being is not thought of as existing in reality as well as being an object of thought, then the being thus thought of is not the supreme being. To exist in reality as well as being an object of thought is to have more being than a mere object of thought has.

To hold before one's mind a correct notion of the supreme being one must make that notion include the note of real existence, over and above being merely an object of thought. In short, to think of the supreme being as merely an object of thought is not to think of the supreme being at all, but of a lesser being.

The argument as stated occurs in Chapter II of Anselm's *Proslogium*. Chapter III restates it, adding another note to

the notion of God that is thus being constructed. It is not
enough to think of the supreme being as one that actually
does exist in reality. Such a being may exist now, but not
in the past or in the future. It may have come into existence
and it may pass away.

Can we think of a being greater than the one just mentioned? Yes, one that cannot *not* exist, one that never comes
into existence and never passes away, because its very nature
is to exist.

Hence, Anselm concludes, if we hold before our minds
the notion of the supreme being, the one being than which
no greater can be thought of, we must at least *think* of that
being as always existing and as incapable of not existing.

I have italicized "think" because Anselm himself would
not be satisfied with the statement I have just made. As he
understood it, his argument led to the conclusion that the
supreme being does in fact exist in reality and must so exist.

Postponing until later my criticism of the mistake made
by Anselm and by certain of his 20th-century defenders, I
wish now to consider whether the so-called "ontological argument" provides us with notes that pagans can employ in
the formulation of a definite description of God. Does the
theoretical construct that is their notion of God include such
notes as (1) the one and only supreme being, (2) which actually does exist in reality, and (3) which cannot not so exist?

These three notes would appear to be compatible with
one another. A theoretical construct involving all three
would, therefore, not be a self-contradictory notion. Nor
does the note of supremacy in being, from which the other
two notes appear to follow, raise any difficulties in itself. Pagans, I think, would not demur at being asked to think of
God as the supreme being, as long as the question of God's
existence remains open.

Just as in the realm of magnitudes or multitudes, we can
think of an infinite extent or an infinite number, than which

no greater can be thought of, so also, in the realm of existence, we can think of a being than which no greater can be thought of. The difficulty, if there is one, is raised by the question whether the second and third note inexorably follow from the first. If we think of (1) the supreme being, must we also think of that supreme being as (2) one that actually does exist in reality and as (3) one that cannot not exist?

Modern philosophers have questioned both (2) and (3), on grounds that I regard as faulty.

Immanuel Kant objected to the transition from (1) to (2) on the grounds that existence is not a predicate and that it adds nothing to the perfection of the subject of which it is predicated. It must, of course, be conceded that the word "exists," in a sentence such as "a president of the United States exists," or such as "horses exist," is not like any other predicate, such as "strong" and "swift" said of horses, or such as "wise" and "courageous" said of a president of the United States. These predicates characterize their subjects, as "exists" does not.

According to Kant, a thing's perfections consist exclusively in the attributes that constitute its nature. Such terms as "strong" or "wise" say something about the nature of the object to which they are applied, and when applied they indicate perfections it possesses. But for Kant the term "exists" does not say anything about the nature of the object of which it is said, and therefore it does not indicate a perfection of that object.

Accordingly, an existent horse or an existent president has no more perfection than a non-existent horse or a non-existent president; whereas a strong and swift horse is a better horse than a weak and slow one; a wise and courageous president is a better president than a foolish and cowardly one.

While "exists" is not an ordinary predicate, since it says

nothing about the nature or character of the subject under consideration, it is, nevertheless, an indispensable predicate. Take, for example, the following two propositions: "Horses are corporeal" and "mermaids are corporeal." Both are true as far as they go, but they do not go far enough. The full truth of the matter requires the following more complex statements: "There are horses in reality *and* all are corporeal"; "There are no mermaids in reality, but if there were, all would be corporeal."

The two prefatory statements—"there are horses in reality" and "there are no mermaids in reality"—express precisely what we mean when we say "horses exist" and "mermaids do not exist." Any stricture against such statements as "horses exist" and "mermaids do not exist" should apply equally to such statements as "there are horses" and "there are no mermaids."

The second part of Kant's criticism is also faulty. Conceding that "exists" is not an ordinary predicate, yet one that we cannot do without unless we are willing to forgo saying that there are horses but there are no mermaids, is it true that something which really exists is in no way superior to that which is purely imaginary or merely an object of thought?

Is not a hundred dollars in my pocket better than an imaginary hundred dollars by virtue of its enabling me to buy things with it? Is not a really existent umbrella or raincoat better than an imaginary one so far as protection from the rain is concerned?

It would certainly appear to be so, and if it is, then why is it not also true to say that God existing in reality is superior to God existing solely as an object of thought? Superior in what way? As having *more* being—not only the being that is possessed by an object of thought, but also the being of that which exists in reality as well.

Having that additional being, does it not also have more

power? Does not a really existent supreme being have the power to do what cannot be done by the supreme being when it is nothing but an object of thought?

My affirmative answer to all these questions removes the criticisms leveled by Kant against the ontological argument, not interpreted as arguing for God's existence (which Kant did not believe could be rationally established), but rather as arguing that (2) and (3) inexorably follow from (1).

Of course, if (2) and (3) do not follow from (1), then the ontological argument also fails as an argument for God's existence as Kant maintained. In my view the ontological argument fails as an argument for God's existence, but notes (2) and (3) do follow from note (1).

Some 20th-century philosophers have espoused Kant's criticisms. They have, in addition, raised a cloud of dust about the word "necessary" as attached to the word "exists." They regard necessity as a purely logical notion, applicable only to propositions, indicating their modality—the kind of truth they have.

For example, the statement "the whole is greater than any of its parts" is a necessary truth: It cannot be otherwise; it is impossible to think of the whole as less than any of its parts. In contrast, "horses are white" is not a necessary truth; it is quite possible for there to be some black and some brown as well as some white horses.

These modern philosophers are quite correct in thinking that no existential proposition—no proposition which affirms the existence of something (there are horses) or which denies the existence of something (there are no mermaids)—can be a necessary proposition. The relation between "exists" as the very special predicate that it is and any subject to which it is applied is never a necessary connection.

The proposition "God exists" may be true, but it is not and cannot be necessarily true. Even though it may be necessary for us to think of the supreme being as one that actually does exist and as one that cannot not exist, we are not thereby compelled to assert either that the supreme being does in fact actually exist or that it is a necessary truth that the supreme being does exist.

Subsequent interpretations of Anselm's ontological argument have introduced the notion of "necessary existence" as equivalent in meaning to the notion of "that which cannot not exist." Accordingly, to say that the supreme being is one that cannot not exist is equivalent to saying that the supreme being is a necessary being or one that has necessary existence.

Another term that is then introduced is "contingent." It is equivalent in meaning to "that which may or may not exist" or "that which comes into existence and passes away," as a necessary being does not.

Modern logicians, insisting that "necessary" and "contingent" are purely logical terms, applicable only to propositions and nothing else, think they have scored a devastating point against the ontological argument. In fact, all they have done is refuse to acknowledge that such terms as "necessary" and "contingent" have been used and can be legitimately used as ontological terms, not solely as logical terms—as properties of being or existence, not solely as properties of propositions.

When we dismiss their criticisms of the ontological argument as groundless, we are not led to endorse it as a proof of God's existence. Quite the contrary! We can see that if the supreme being must be thought of as one that cannot not exist, then the supreme being must be thought of as a necessary being. Even if modern logicians were to take off their blinders and admit an ontological as well as a logical use of the word "necessary," they would not be carried by that admission to the conclusion that there exists in reality something corresponding to our constructed notion of a necessary being.

Nor would they be carried to what they rightly regard

as an objectionable conclusion; namely, that the proposition "God exists" expresses a necessary truth. That it does not do, even if the proposition is true, which is still open to question.

While I think I have satisfactorily removed the modern objections to Anselm's ontological argument (interpreted as a first step toward the formulation of a definite description of God), I also think that there is a better way of undertaking that task.

I will set forth that way in the next chapter, as a second step toward arriving at the theoretical construct which is our notion of God. It will retain the notes that Anselm introduced, such as "supreme being," "real existence," and "necessary existence," but it will enable us to add other notes and to understand Anselm's three notes better.

CHAPTER 9

How to Formulate a Definite Description of God: Second Step

IN UNDERTAKING TO DESCRIBE the existence of God, Anselm proceeded in the manner of a Christian theologian who himself believed in God and wished to understand what he believed in.

As we have seen, the argument that Anselm used has been the subject of controversy over many centuries because an illicit proof of God's existence always seems to be lurking in the background.

I shall, therefore, propose a different procedure, one more appropriate to a purely philosophical approach to the question, intended primarily for 20th-century pagans. It is a procedure which can be undertaken and considered in the darkness of unbelief and does not become questionable when so considered.

To formulate a definite description of God, let us undertake to answer the following question:

IF God, or IF the supreme being, really exists, what is the existence of God, or of the supreme being, like?

It is clear from the start, and should not be overlooked or forgotten, that however we answer this question, no answer that we give will lead logically to the conclusion that God really does exist, that is, has existence outside the mind. The question introduced by the word "IF" is purely hypothetical and protects us from ever supposing that the answers we give can do more than help us construct a notion of God— the theoretical construct we need in order to go on to inquire whether anything corresponding to that notion does in fact really exist.

I would call attention also to the fact that in formulating the question in this way I have allowed the phrase "the supreme being" to serve as a synonym for "God." I have done so because I think Anselm provided us with a first step toward formulating a definite description of God when he asked us to think of a being than which no greater can be thought of.

If, after we have done everything we can to identify the object we have in mind when we think of God, we can still think of a greater, we would, in my judgment, realize that we had not been thinking of God but of something less than God. Hence, from this point on, any notes we introduce in the course of constructing our notion of God must be notes that are compatible with Anselm's initial note, which identifies God as an object that we must think of as the supreme being.

We cannot entertain the notion of the supreme being without thinking of that being as having real existence. This second note is inseparable from the first note that Anselm introduced in his *Proslogium*, Chapter II, when he asked us to think of a being than which no greater can be thought of. I will, therefore, include both of these notes in my further effort to construct a definite description of God.

There are three possible answers to the hypothetical question I have asked—three and only three, since each answer excludes both of the others and all three together are exhaustive:

1. God's existence is totally unlike the existence of all the things the real existence of which we know either by direct acquaintance or by inference from empirical evidence.
2. God's existence is essentially and totally like the existence of all these other things.
3. God's existence is both like and unlike the existence of everything else that really exists.

Before I undertake to show why the third of these answers is, in my judgment, the right one, let me offer a few words of comment and clarification with regard to all three.

In the first place, all three call for a comparison of God, as an object of thought (one which may or may not be more than an object of thought), with the things of nature—the physical individuals that are components of the cosmos as a whole. These, too, are objects of thought but, as our wording of the three statements indicates, they are also more than that. Many of them are perceptual objects, which we know by direct acquaintance. Some of them we know by inference from empirical evidence. However we come to know of their existence, they are all objects of thought that do not exist in our minds alone, but exist also in reality; that is, outside our minds and when no one is thinking of them.

In the second place, though we will begin by considering how God's existence is like or unlike the things of this world, the real existence of which is somehow known to us, we cannot complete our inquiry without considering how God's existence is like or unlike the existence of the cosmos as a whole.

In the third place, I must remind the reader that, in Chapter 7, I showed why it was not inconsistent to say that God is like other objects while still insisting that God is unclassifiable. Hence the unclassifiability of God does not prevent us from offering the second and third of the foregoing statements as possible answers to the question we are considering.

I will now attempt to explain why, of the three statements about God's existence being like or unlike that of everything else which exists, we are compelled to choose the third and reject the other two. The third, it will be remembered, asserts that God's existence is both like and unlike the existence of everything else that really exists.

The reason why we are compelled to choose this one of the three alternatives is that it is the one we are left with when we have found that we cannot say either (1) that God's existence is totally unlike that of everything else which really exists, or (2) that God's existence is essentially like that of everything else.

We cannot say (1) that God's existence is totally unlike that of everything else. To do so is incompatible with our having already included the note of real existence in our initial formulation of a definite description of God. Furthermore, if we were to say that God's real existence is totally unlike the real existence of everything else we know to exist, we would be using the term "real existence" in a completely equivocal manner.

That would leave us entirely blank about the meaning of "real existence" when we speak of God as having real existence. We should not use words that have no sense for us. There is no point in saying that we must think of God as having real existence if that is a totally senseless remark, as it turns out to be if God's real existence is totally unlike the real existence of everything else.

When we affirm the real existence of God or anything else, we are affirming that the object in question exists outside the mind and when it is not being thought of. It is, in short, not merely an object of thought.

Since we can think of God as having real existence in a sense that is not totally unlike the real existence that you and I possess, we must reject the first of the three answers. The rejected answer is, in addition, incompatible with one of the notes we adopted from Anselm's argument when we realized that we cannot think of God as the supreme being without also thinking of God as really existing.

The second alternative must also be rejected. Here the reason is quite different. To say that God's existence is essentially like that of everything else known by us to exist is tantamount to saying that God's existence is physical, material, or corporeal, and that, consequently, it is a mode of existence which can be known to us either by direct perceptual acquaintance or by scientific inference from empirical evidence.

What is wrong with saying this? The simple indisputable fact is that the existence of God has never been a subject of scientific inquiry. It has never been supposed that the problem of whether or not God exists can be solved by the means and methods at the disposal of the experimental or empirical natural sciences.

Why not? Because the means and methods of natural science are applicable only to physical, material, or corporeal objects and God is not a physical, material, or corporeal object.

"How's that again?" or "Not so fast," some of my more critical readers may interject at this point. In saying that the existence of God cannot be an object of scientific investigation because God is immaterial or incorporeal, have I not assumed the very point that needs to be established?

The fact that natural science so far has not used its means and methods to investigate the existence of God does not preclude the possibility of its doing so in the future, by techniques not now imaginable by us. Hence, there must be some other reason for thinking that God cannot be essentially like the physical things of this world, known by us to exist.

Another line of reasoning is available. It takes its departure from our understanding of the cosmos as the totality of material or corporeal things and all physical occurrences and processes. As a totality, it is all-embracing. Nothing can be physical, material, or corporeal and exist outside the cosmos, for if it did, the cosmos would not be the totality of all such things.

Now, if we think of God as physical, material, or corporeal, God must be thought of either (1) as a part of the physical cosmos, or (2) as identical with the cosmos as a whole. Or, (3), the cosmos must be thought of as part of God.

The cosmos cannot be a part of God and remain the totality of physical things, occurrences, and processes. A part of something that is itself physical or material cannot be the totality of all physical or material things. This eliminates the third alternative.

God cannot be thought of as a part of the physical cosmos and also be thought of as the supreme being; for then the physical cosmos as a whole, which includes God as a part of itself, would be greater than God. This eliminates the first alternative.

We are left with the second alternative—that God is identical with the physical cosmos as the totality of all physical things, occurrences, and processes. But the physical cosmos, vast totality that it is, is certainly not that than which no greater can be thought of. Hence, if we identify God with the physical cosmos, we are no longer thinking of God as the supreme being—that than which no greater can be thought of.

The elimination of all three alternatives as impossible brings us to the conclusion that God cannot be thought of as physical, material, or corporeal. That being so, we cannot say that God is essentially like the things of the physical world, which are physical, material, or corporeal.

Having rejected the first and second alternatives, we are left with the third—that God's existence is both like and unlike that of other objects of thought the real existence of which we know either by direct perceptual acquaintance or by inference from empirical evidence.

How unlike? We have already answered this question. It is unlike in every respect that is relevant to the way in which we know or ascertain the real existence of other things. The real existence of God, being immaterial and incorporeal, must be imperceptible. It must also be unascertainable by scientific inference from empirical evidence, that is, evidence that we have through sense perception.

Anything, from horses and diamonds to electrons and black holes, the real existence of which is either directly perceptible or detectable from empirical evidence is physical, material, or corporeal. It exists either in the way that bodies exist, or in the way that the physical actions or movements of bodies exist, or it is the material aspect of a body, or, as in the case of the cosmos as a whole, it is a vast congeries of bodies in interaction with one another.

The briefest way to sum this up is to say that God's existence is totally immaterial and non-physical. If everything physical is natural, if physical existence is natural existence, then another way of saying the same thing is that God's existence—IF God does exist in reality—is supernatural.

How like? Clearly, it is not enough to say that God, like every other object of thought, may or may not exist. Every object of thought is a possible existent, in the sense that it may actually exist, that is, exist outside the mind and when no one is thinking of it. Our concern here is with the actual, not the possible, existence of God. Our question is: How, IF God does actually exist, does God's existence resemble that of everything else that actually exists?

Things can be alike in two ways, not one. They can be either (a) univocally alike or (b) analogically alike. Let me explain the distinction between these two modes of likeness.

Things are univocally alike when the word which names their likeness is said of them in exactly the same sense. For example, when we say "chair" of this chair, that chair, or any other chair, without any change of meaning, we are using that word univocally, and the chairs spoken of are all alike in exactly the same sense of the word.

The exact opposite of univocal likeness is the unlikeness of things that are equivocally named, such as an enclosure for pigs and a writing instrument, both of which are called "pens."

Intermediate between these two extremes is a likeness that is fused with unlikeness—a likeness that is intrinsically diversified in the very respect in which the like things are said to be alike. Such likeness is called "analogical."

Whereas two things are univocally alike when the word that names their likeness is applied to them in exactly the same sense, two things are analogically alike when the word that names their likeness is applied to them in a sense that is diversified by the intrinsic differences between them.

When we say of God and other things that both really exist, we are not saying that both have "real existence" in exactly the same sense of that term. If we were, we could have chosen the second of the three alternatives; namely, that the existence of God and that of other things is essentially alike.

Nor can we be saying that the sense in which we speak of

God as really existing and the sense in which we speak of other things as really existing have nothing in common. If that were what we were saying, we could have chosen the first of the three alternatives: namely, that the existence of God and of other things is totally unlike.

Hence we must be saying that, IF God exists as other things exist in reality, in the sense that they have existence outside the mind—as more than objects of thought, and even when no one is thinking of them—such real existence is intrinsically diversified by the difference between corporeal and incorporeal, between material and immaterial, between physical and spiritual, and between natural and supernatural.

The likeness between the real existence of God (IF God exists in reality) and the real existence of the things of this world (the existence of which is known to us either by perceptual acquaintance or by inference from evidence accessible to sense perception) is, therefore, analogical, not univocal.

The procedure we have been employing has now brought us to the point at which we can assert, not that God really exists, but that real existence is the only positive note in the notion of God that we are constructing; and that this one positive note must be intrinsically qualified by all the negative notes that represent the essential unlikeness between the real existence of God and that of everything else.

Our choice of the third alternative requires us to answer the question "IF God exists, what is God's real existence like?" by saying that it is analogically like that of the things of this world the real existence of which we know in one way or another. We can now see that such analogical likeness consists in the intrinsic qualification of the positive note of real existence by all the negative notes that represent the essential unlikeness between the real existence of God and that of everything else.

So far, the procedure we have been employing has identified the object of thought, to which we have given the name "God," by two descriptive notes: (1) the supreme being; (2) having real existence in an analogical sense of that term. If we had been identifying "Hamlet" as an object of thought, we might have said: (a) a person in a play by Shakespeare; (b) lacking real existence in any sense of that term.

In addition to those two notes, which Anselm provided, we have put into our definite description a number of negative notes not mentioned by Anselm in Chapters II and III of his *Proslogium*, as follows: (3) immaterial, incorporeal, non-physical; and (4) consequently non-natural or supernatural.

On further thought, one other negative note suggests itself. The things of this world are all finite, all limited in quantity. But they are finite in another sense because each is a particular individual.

As particular individuals, each of the things of this world has a limited existence, in two ways. First, each is limited in its existence to the kind of existence that a given kind of thing has. By this limitation, it is precluded from having the kind of existence that is possessed by other kinds of things. Second, each is limited in its existence to the existence it has as just one particular instance of that kind of thing. By this limitation, it is precluded from having the existence possessed by other particular instances of the same kind. Both limitations are contractions of its existence and make it finite.

God, as we have seen, is unclassifiable—not a particular instance of any kind. Though we must think of God as a unique, singular entity, we cannot think of God as a particular individual belonging to a kind or class of which he is just one instance. Hence, as compared with the things of this world, which are particular individuals having only a finite existence, God must be thought of as having an unlimited, uncontracted, *not* finite, or infinite, existence.

If, at this point, readers protest that they cannot understand what it means to say that something has infinite existence, my only answer is to remind them that "infinite" is a negative, not a positive, word. The same is true of "immaterial," "incorporeal," "non-physical," and even "supernatural," which is equivalent in meaning to "non-natural." In all these instances, our understanding consists solely in negating what we understand by the positive correlates of these words. To say that we must think of God as having an infinite existence is to say no more than that we must think of God as *not* having a finite existence.

Can we now add one more note to our description of God as a unique, singular object of thought? The note in question is the note included in Anselm's analytical reasoning about what is involved in the notion of God—the note expressed by the words "cannot not exist." If we must think of God not only as having real existence, but also as being incapable of not existing, then the note to be added to our description of God can be expressed positively by the words "necessary existence," or by the statement that God must be thought of as a necessary being.

The meaning of "necessary" as applied to existence or being would also appear to be negative rather than positive. It lies in our understanding that such a being does not come into existence, endure for a while, and then pass out of existence. In contrast, we used the word "contingent," as applied to existence or being, in a positive sense, signifying that the beings we call contingent do come into existence, endure for a while, and pass away.

Our method of constructing a definite description of God by comparing that object of thought with the things of this world known by us to exist arrives at the same conclusion that Anselm's analysis reached.

The things of this world are all contingent beings. That their existence is contingent is manifested by the fact of their temporal finitude. They have existence only for the time during which they endure—from the moment they come into existence until the time they pass away. If we must think of God as the supreme being, having an infinite and supernatural existence, in which respects his existence is analogically like (that is, like-and-unlike) the existence of other things, then we must also think of God as having necessary existence. God must be thought of as a necessary rather than as a contingent being.

We can arrive at the same conclusion in another way, which is confirmatory. All the things of this world are not only particular individuals, but they are also parts of the natural order—parts or components of an all-embracing physical cosmos. God, not being corporeal or physical, cannot be a part of the cosmos. The individual things that are parts of the physical cosmos depend for their existence upon the operation of natural causes *and* conditions—not only the causes that are responsible for their coming into existence, but also the conditions that sustain their existence while they endure.

It is, therefore, appropriate to describe the things of this world as having a dependent, conditioned, and caused existence. If we must think of God's existence as being like-and-unlike the existence of the things of this world, we must think of God as having an independent, unconditioned, and uncaused existence. To say this is just another way of saying that God has a necessary existence.

If God's existence were not thought of as independent, unconditioned, and uncaused (all these words, by the way, are negative in their significance), we would not be thinking of God as the supreme being. Not only must we think of the supreme being as one that really exists, but also as one the existence of which is necessary in the negative sense of being independent, unconditioned, and uncaused.

That which is independent, unconditioned, and uncaused in its existence has its existence in, through, and from itself. If we summarize what has just been said by use of the Latin phrase "*a se*," we can employ the infrequently used word "aseity" to signify the note that we have added to our description of God as an object of thought. In contrast, the things of this world, the existence of which is contingent, dependent, conditioned, and caused, do not have their existence in, through, and from themselves. They do not have aseity.

Two further negative notes would appear to follow from what has just been said. The contingent things of this world, having a dependent, conditioned, and caused existence, enduring only for a finite period of time, are all temporal and mutable. They are subject to change while they exist as well as having existence only for a time. If we must think of God as a necessary being, having an independent, unconditioned, and uncaused existence, and, above all, as having aseity (existence in, through, and from himself), we must also think of God as immutable and non-temporal.

God is sometimes spoken of as eternal, but the word "eternal" has two meanings: (1) a positive meaning, which is expressed by the words "everlasting in duration, always existing"; and (2) a negative meaning, which is expressed by the words "non-temporal and immutable." It is primarily in the negative sense that we should speak of God as eternal. That negative sense does not exclude the fact that we must think of God as everlasting or always existing (not coming into being or passing away). In thinking of God as everlasting in existence, we must also think of God's everlasting existence as immutable—as unchanging.

Why? Because that which has aseity cannot be affected by anything outside itself. That which does not have aseity, that which is mutable or changing, is affected by what lies outside itself—by causes or conditions that operate or impinge upon it. Hence to say that God has aseity is not only to say that God is immutable, but also to say that God is in no way affected or altered by the existence or non-existence of the cosmos as a whole, totally outside of which God has independent existence.

So far we have been describing God by comparing that

object of thought with the things of this world known by us to exist. These things are parts or components of the cosmos, also known by us to exist. Some of the characteristics we have assigned to them, we cannot assign to the cosmos as a whole.

Unlike the things that are components of it, the cosmos as a whole, being a totality, is not a part of anything else. Furthermore, in the light of the assumption that we found it necessary to make at the very beginning—that the cosmos has an everlasting existence, that it is a world without beginning or end—we must say of the cosmos, as we say of God, that it neither comes into being nor passes away.

It would appear, therefore, that two properties which enter into our notion of God also enter into our notion of the cosmos. We must describe both as (1) everlasting in existence, and (2) independent or unconditioned in existence, at least to the extent that neither exists as part of a whole upon which it depends for its existence or which conditions its existence. Further, since we must say that the cosmos is everlasting in existence, neither coming into being nor passing away, it would appear that we should say (3) that the cosmos, like God, has necessary rather than contingent existence.

Why, then, do we not identfy our notion of God with our notion of the cosmos, as pantheists would have us do?

There are many reasons for not doing so: first, because the cosmos is mutable, ever-changing; second, because the cosmos is material, corporeal, physical; third, and most important, because we are not compelled to think of the cosmos as the supreme being, than which no greater can be thought of.

This last reason might be further supported by a point that cannot be fully explained until later; namely, that as we understand the universe which now exists and of which we are parts, it is not the only *possible* universe. It is, therefore, a particular universe, one instance of the class that includes all possible universes. It does *not*, therefore, have infinite existence and is, therefore, *not* the supreme being. Hence the cosmos is *not* God.

If the cosmos that now exists never came into being out of nothing, why we do not say of it that, like God, it is not only independent and unconditioned because it is not a part of some greater whole, but also that it is independent and unconditioned because it is *uncaused*? Why do we not say of the cosmos that, like God, it has aseity—that, like God, it has its existence *in, from, and through itself*?

That is a very difficult question to answer here. I will attempt to answer it later. Here all I can say is that we *may or may not* think of the cosmos as having aseity, whereas we *must* think of God as having aseity. Again, the reader may ask why.

If we must think of God as having necessary existence or aseity because we must think of the supreme being as one that cannot not exist and so does not come into existence or pass away, why should we not, for the same reason, think of the cosmos as having aseity or necessary existence? It, too, does not come into existence or pass away.

If we must think of God as having an uncaused existence because we must think of God as having an everlasting existence, why should we not, for the same reason, think of the cosmos as having an uncaused existence?

The only answer that I can give here may appear to be a weak one, but it is as strong as I can make it at this point in our inquiry. Granted that a cosmos which does not come into being does not need a creator or exnihilator—a cause that brings it into existence out of nothing. In this respect, an everlasting cosmos is uncaused. But are we not also compelled to ask whether an everlasting cosmos may not need a cause of its continuing existence at every moment of time that it endures everlastingly?

If, at this point in our inquiry, we were to answer that

question negatively, we would foreclose any further inquiry. It must be left open for further inquiry to discover whether God's existence needs to be posited in order to explain the continuing existence of the everlasting cosmos.

To say that the continuing existence of the everlasting cosmos does not need a cause is tantamount to saying that, whatever notion we finally form of God as an object of thought, we do not have to assert that, in addition to being an object of thought, God really exists.

In order to go on with this inquiry concerning the existence of God, we must, therefore, at this point say only that the everlasting cosmos *may or may not* need a cause of its continuing existence.

Let me now summarize the notion of God that we have constructed, which provides us with a definite description of God as a unique, singular object of thought. According to that definite description, when we think of God, we are thinking of the supreme being, having real existence in an analogical sense because that existence is (1) immaterial, incorporeal, non-physical, non-temporal, immutable, and also (2) necessary, (3) independent, unconditioned, uncaused, and (4) infinite.

Two things, not one, remain to be seen, and they are intimately connected with one another. One is whether we must think of the cosmos as independent, unconditioned, and uncaused. The other will follow from the answer we give to that question. It is whether there exists in reality anything which corresponds to the notion of God that we have formed.

Only if we have some reason for thinking that God exists not only as an object of thought, but also in reality, quite apart from our thinking, do we have reason for believing in God's real existence.

CHAPTER 10

On Inferring Existence

ALL PROPOSITIONS or judgments which assert that something is the case fall into two main groups. They are either existential or non-existential. They either do or do not assert the existence of something.

When we say "mermaids have tails" and "horses have tails" we are saying something about the characteristics of mermaids and horses, not that there are horses or mermaids. Such judgments must be expressed in additional statements to that effect, either by saying "horses exist" or by saying what is strictly equivalent, "there are horses."

Existential propositions can be further subdivided. "Horses exist" or "there are horses" exemplifies one type of existential proposition. This type asserts the existence of entities, *in the plural*, which are instances of a class that has been defined.

Defining the class to which horses or the class to which

mermaids belong does not tell us whether or not that class has any members in the real world. If there are none, then we say that the class is a null or empty class, as are all classes the members of which are, like mermaids, nothing more than imaginary objects or objects of thought. Only if we know that particular instances of the class do in fact exist are we in a position to declare that the class is not empty or null. Such knowledge is expressed, for example, in the *general* existential proposition "horses exist" or "there are horses."

The other type of existential proposition is singular, not general. This type asserts or denies the existence in reality of a unique, singular object, designated by a proper name or a definite description. For example, we can say that Hamlet, the leading character in a play by Shakespeare, did not exist at the time that Shakespeare wrote about him. We can say that Shakespeare was real—that he existed in the era of Queen Elizabeth I. Such existential propositions may be in the past tense, like the foregoing statements, or they may be in the present tense ("There is no king of France at the present moment") or in the future tense ("The house for which these are the architectural plans will exist on this spot next year").

The proposition "God exists" is an existential proposition of the second type. Yet it is also like the general existential proposition "electrons exist" or "there are electrons," because it asserts the existence in reality of an object of thought (the notion of which is a theoretical construct)—an object of thought that is not also a perceptual object. But, unlike "electrons exist," the proposition "God exists" asserts the existence of a unique singular that is not a particular instance of a certain class of objects.

Among all existential propositions, the proposition "God exists" stands alone. For the reasons given above, it is a unique proposition, even as the word "God" is unique among proper names. Nevertheless, as we will see, the proposition resembles all other existential propositions in two negative respects: (1) It is *not* self-evidently true or false; (2) it is *not* necessarily true or false.

These two considerations—that "God" is unique among proper names and that "God exists" is unique among existential propositions—must control any attempt to argue for God's existence. Not only must we, as we have already done, produce a definite description of the unique object the real existence of which is in question; we must also understand that the way in which we argue for or try to infer God's existence must be somewhat different from the way in which we try to argue for or infer the existence of any other object or objects the existence of which is in question.

I have used the words "try to argue for or infer" rather than the word "prove" or "demonstrate" because the latter words, in my judgment, are much too strong when we are concerned with the real existence of imperceptible physical entities, such as electrons, neutrinos, mesons, or black holes, or with the real existence of God. We should confine our use of "prove" or "demonstrate" to mathematical reasoning.

In the first book of his *Elements of Geometry*, Euclid demonstrates the existence of equilateral triangles by proving that they can be constructed in the mathematical, not physical, space that his postulates define. Existence proofs in geometry, or other branches of mathematics, are demonstrations, but arguments in experimental physics for the existence of nuclear particles and arguments in theology for the existence of God are not. If they are cogent and persuasive, they represent reasonable inferences, but they fall short of the kind of certitude that should attach to a conclusion which is proved or demonstrated.

The 18th-century Scottish philosopher David Hume was correct in thinking that no proposition about a matter of fact or real existence can be proved or demonstrated. But it is certainly not correct to say that we cannot cogently argue for the truth of such propositions, or arrive at the truth of such propositions by reasonable inferences that justify us in affirming them with something less than the certitude achieved by mathematical proofs or demonstrations.

Argument and inference are not always involved in our having knowledge of the real existence of particular instances of a class of objects or of some unique, singular object. We know by direct perceptual acquaintance that there are horses. We know, similarly, that a certain friend of ours exists or that there is a certain building on a certain corner of this city.

Knowing the existence of that friend, by your direct acquaintance with him, may lead you to infer the past existence of his grandparents, who no longer exist and with whom you cannot be acquainted perceptually. The valid generalization, which underlies this inference, is simply that every human being has grandparents who were alive before he was born.

These objects, the real existence of which we cannot know by direct perceptual acquaintance, can be known by us to exist only through inference. Such inference is not always of the type exemplified by the inference concerning the prior existence of grandparents. However, this much is true of all existential inferences. What they have in common is the presence of an existential assertion among the premises of the reasoning through which the inference takes place.

If you had not known of the existence of your friend by direct perceptual acquaintance, you would have had insufficient grounds for inferring the existence of your friend's grandparents, even though the generalization about the prior existence of grandparents for every human being is true.

Existential inferences divide into two types. They are either (1) inferences to the real existence of a unique singular, such as your friend's grandfather, or (2) inferences to the real existence of particular instances of a class of entities—one or another kind of elementary particle in nuclear physics.

Let us consider the second type first. Here the governing rule of inference is stated by a famous rule of thought, first formulated by a 14th-century British philosopher, William of Ockham. Ockham declared that we are justified in positing or asserting the real existence of unobserved or unobservable entities if—and *only* if—their real existence is indispensable for the explanation of observed phenomena.

Without such justification, we should refrain from positing the real existence of objects of thought that we hold before our minds by means of theoretical constructs, as in the case of elementary particles or black holes. Ockham's razor is the negative aspect of Ockham's rule: Its cutting edge deletes from reality those hypothetical entities which we are not justified in positing.

Inferences that are governed by Ockham's rule also conform to the general principle that is applicable to all existential inferences (the premises must include at least one existential assertion). In nuclear physics, the required existential assertion takes the form of acknowledging the existence of certain experimental observations—certain experimentally observed phenomena that call for explanation.

If the explanation called for requires us to posit the existence of a certain type of elementary particle, on the ground that the phenomena can be explained in no other way, we then have reasonable grounds for inferring that there do exist in reality certain hypothetical entities of which we have formed a theoretical construct.

Unless and until an inference of this type is based on observed facts and is justified by conformity to Ockham's rule, the hypothetical entities of which we have formed a theoretical construct remain purely hypothetical. They remain ideal entities—objects of thought, or merely possible existences not yet known by us to exist in reality.

Let us now turn to the first type of existential inference. Here the object in question is a unique singular, for example, the Loch Ness monster. If the Loch Ness monster exists, it should at least be possible for us to know of its existence by direct perceptual acquaintance. Until that possibility is realized for us, our only way of knowing whether it exists is by inference from evidence of one kind or another.

That evidence may take the form of testimony on the part of some witness who claims that he saw the monster; or it may take the form of an observation on our part of traces or effects that we interpret as having resulted from the movements or actions of the monster. In the case of another hypothetical object, the Abominable Snowman, such traces may be observed footprints in the Himalayan snow.

We all recognize how tenuous inferences of this sort may be, either because we question the credibility of a witness whose testimony we have heard, or because the interpretation of the observed evidence may seem farfetched.

However, inferences of this sort need not be tenuous and weak. In courts of law, criminals are convicted on the basis of testimonial and circumstantial evidence that leads a jury to bring in a verdict of guilty beyond a reasonable doubt. The jury's verdict of guilty as charged asserts an existential proposition—that the prisoner at the bar did in fact perform a certain criminal act at a certain time and place.

Not all trials of questions of fact before a judicial tribunal involving judge and jury require the degree of probative force expressed by the words "proof beyond a reasonable doubt," which is always less than the certitude achieved in what is *genuinely* proof (a mathematical demonstration). In civil as opposed to criminal cases, the requirement may call for a verdict supported by a preponderance of the evidence. When a jury renders the latter verdict, it is saying that the existential proposition it affirms has greater probability than its opposite.

Sometimes, in addition to testimonial and circumstantial evidence, existential inferences by judicial tribunals are based on direct perceptual acquaintance with traces from the past, as when the jury is shown an exhibit in the form of a signed document or a used weapon. Historical research employs exactly the same kind of existential inference as that which occurs in trials of issues of fact before judicial tribunals. Historical research concerning the existence of certain events in the past, or certain particulars, may employ the testimony of witnesses, but it usually relies more heavily on observable traces from the past, in the form of monuments, archaeological remains, and documents.

What is common to all such existential inferences is their employment of empirical generalizations to infer, either from observed testimony or from observed traces, the existence of the particular fact in question. What is miscalled "circumstantial evidence" is not evidence at all. It is nothing but the appeal to such generalizations for the purpose of making an inference—as, for example, the appeal made to the generalization that all human beings have grandparents when we infer that the friend we know by acquaintance had grandparents alive at some prior time.

In this respect, such inferences differ from the type of existential inference that occurs in nuclear physics or cosmology. There it is Ockham's rule rather than an empirical generalization to which we appeal in arguing from observed facts to the existence of a fact in question. There, too, the fact in question is not a unique singular, such as Caesar's crossing the Rubicon on a certain date, or the criminal action with which the prisoner at the bar is charged. Instead, the fact in question is the existence in reality of instances of a certain class of entities, defined by a theoretical construct.

However, in both types of existential inference, the conclusion is not established with certitude, but only to a certain degree of probability, or, as it is said in courts of law, either by a preponderance of the evidence or beyond a reasonable doubt.

CHAPTER 11

On Inferring God's Existence

W<small>E HAVE SEEN IN EARLIER CHAPTERS</small> why the word "God" is unique among proper names and why the proposition "God exists" is unique among existential assertions. I will now explain why and how arguments for or inferences to God's existence are unique among existential arguments or inferences.

The quickest way to point out that uniqueness is to call attention to the fact that, on the one hand, inferring God's existence is like inferring the real existence of certain nuclear particles or black holes, and, on the other hand, it is also like inferring the existence of some singular fact by the method of historical research or that of judicial proceedings.

What inferring God's existence has in common with inferring the existence of certain nuclear particles is that, in both cases, we are concerned with the real existence of something corresponding to a theoretical construct that we have formed in order to hold the object in mind. The entity in question is not directly observable by us. In both cases, Ockham's rule governs the inference.

We are not justified in positing a certain type of elementary particle unless asserting its existence is indispensable for the explanation of experimentally observed phenomena. We are not justified in positing the existence of God unless affirming God's existence is indispensable for the explanation of . . . of what?

That question calls attention at once to a fundamental difference between inferring the existence of a certain type of nuclear particle and inferring the existence of God. In the latter case, it is not experimentally observed phenomena that call for explanation, but rather the existence of individual things which are parts of the cosmos or the existence of the cosmos as a whole.

There are other differences as well. In nuclear physics, the point of departure usually is some experimentally observed phenomenon that is novel. Its novelty calls for a new theoretical construct, devised to explain the experimental data. If the explanation succeeds, scientists are justified in affirming the existence in reality of entities corresponding to the class of objects they have in mind. In theology, we begin with the theoretical construct which is our definite description of God, and only then do we ask whether we have grounds for inferring that something corresponding to that theoretical construct exists in reality.

Still another difference should be noted. It lies in the fact that a proposition which asserts that a certain type of nuclear particle exists can be subsequently falsified by additional experimental observations. According to a widely honored view in the philosophy of science, only propositions that can be falsified by empirical evidence are empirical propositions. The proposition "God exists" cannot be falsi-fied by the discovery of any facts not already known to us. It is, therefore, not an empirical proposition.

The foregoing paragraphs show that inferring God's ex-istence is both like and unlike inferring the existence of certain nuclear particles or of black holes. Inferring God's existence is also both like and unlike the kind of existential inference which occurs in historical research and judicial trials of questions of fact.

The likeness resides in the fact that the question under consideration concerns the existence of a unique singular— the occurrence of a certain event in historical research or judicial proceedings; the reality of God in theological in-quiry. However, in historical research or in judicial pro-ceedings, the event in question is one that could have been observed by someone and, in many cases, was so observed, by witnesses whose testimony was considered. Not so in theological inquiry. Here the object the existence of which is in question is beyond observation by anyone; and in this respect it is like certain nuclear particles or black holes, with which we do not have direct perceptual acquaintance.

In the light of all these comparisons which reveal the spe-cial character of arguments or inferences about God's exis-tence, we are now in a position to see what is involved in any sound theological argument or inference.

First of all, it involves the principle of causality. This principle underlies Ockham's rule. What is to be explained is always taken to be an effect, the explanation of which takes the form of positing its cause or causes. If the effect to be explained exists, the cause that explains it exists.

Second, it involves the more comprehensive principle, known as the principle of sufficient reason: Everything that exists or happens has a reason for its existing or happening either (a) in itself or (b) in something else.

To say that everything which exists has a cause would be

tantamount to denying God's existence; for, as we have seen, God must be described as having aseity, which means that God's existence, IF God does exist, is uncaused.

However, to say that everything which exists has a reason for its existing, either (a) in itself or (b) in something else, is not incompatible with affirming God's existence. The aseity of the supreme being is equivalent to its having the reason for its existence in itself. Only that which exists in, from, or through another has the reason for its existence in another.

Third, like existential inferences in experimental physics, in historical research, and in judicial proceedings, existential inferences in theology fall short of achieving the certitude attainable in mathematical demonstrations or proofs. If we are able to show that we have reasonable grounds for believing in God's existence, that belief will have for us a degree of probable truth, somewhat akin to what is described as being "beyond a reasonable doubt" or as resulting from "a preponderance of the evidence."

Two characteristics of all other existential propositions also characterize the proposition "God exists," and have a bearing on attempts to argue for the truth of that proposition.

No existential proposition can be self-evidently true or necessarily true. When we have direct perceptual acquaintance with a particular individual, the existence of that individual is evident to us, but the proposition which asserts that the individual exists is not self-evident, nor is its truth necessary.

Self-evident propositions are propositions which we know to be true directly from our understanding of their component terms, not by a process of reasoning or inference. For example, our understanding of physical *wholes* and *parts* makes the proposition "physical wholes are always greater than their component parts" self-evidently true to us. Not only true, but necessarily true, because the opposite is impossible. We simply cannot think of physical parts as being greater than the whole to which they belong.

There is no existential proposition like the proposition about wholes and parts. Whatever notion we may hold of the subject of an existential proposition, we are not compelled by our understanding of it to assert that something corresponding to it exists in reality. It is always possible that something which we think exists does not in fact exist. Its non-existence is not impossible as it is impossible—in reality as well as in thought—for the quantity of a part to exceed the quantity of the whole to which it belongs.

Even when existential propositions are true, they are never necessarily true, as the proposition about wholes and parts is necessarily true because the opposite is impossible. We can say that something necessarily exists, but to say that is not to say that the proposition which asserts the existence of the thing in question is itself necessarily true.

When we affirm the existence of anything, we can do so in three ways: (1) We can assert simply that it does in fact exist; (2) we can assert that it exists contingently, because it may also not exist; (3) we can assert that it must exist, that it exists necessarily. But whichever of these three things we say, the truth of the proposition that asserts existence is not a necessary truth.

Philosophers who think that Anselm's ontological argument has validity as an existential argument would agree with everything that has just been said about existential propositions not being self-evidently or necessarily true—with one striking exception, which is the proposition "God exists." For them the uniqueness of this exceptional proposition consists mainly in the fact that, though it is existential, it is also self-evidently and necessarily true.

If their opinion were correct, there would, of course, be no need for any argument or inference that proceeds by reasoning to try to establish the truth of the proposition

"God exists." What is self-evident does not need to be established by reasoning.

However, in my judgment, their view is not correct. To the question whether the proposition "God exists" is self-evident, Aquinas responded by saying: "Yes, self-evident to God, but not to us." But he did not fully explain why it is not self-evident to us.

The explanation lies in the fact that we can never pass directly from any notion we have in our minds to an assertion that there is something in reality which corresponds to that notion. This holds even for the notion of God as the supreme being and, therefore, one that not only exists in reality, but also one that cannot not exist, and so necessarily exists.

Contrary to the opinion of the philosophers who think that Anselm's argument establishes God's existence with almost mathematical certitude, I hold that there can be no objection to asking whether there exists in reality anything that corresponds to the definite description that we have formed of God as an object of thought, nor is there any contradiction in denying that God exists in reality.

In Chapter 9, we arrived at a definite description of God, one that includes the three notes involved in the description that Anselm arrived at by a different method. The method we employed took its point of departure from a hypothetical question: "IF God exists, what is God's existence like?"

Our answer to this question included saying that, unlike the existence of the things of this world known by us to exist, God's existence is necessary, not contingent. Of God, we *must* say that God *must* exist. Since this is part of an answer to the hypothetical question with which we began, it did not then and should not now lead us to the conclusion that, because we *must* think of God as a necessary being, God in fact not only does exist, but also *must* exist.

The first "must" does not lead to the second. It is quite

possible that there is nothing in reality that corresponds to our thought of a being which we cannot think of as supreme unless we also think of it as having real and also necessary existence.

At the risk of belaboring the point, I wish to be sure that my dismissal of Anselm's argument as having existential validity is clear. I hope I can finally dispose of a claim that has been moot for centuries.

In formulating a definite description of God, we attach meaning to the word "God" as naming an object of thought. Doing just that asserts nothing. Naming or describing an object is not asserting.

When Anselm discovered what was involved in holding before one's mind the notion of the supreme being (that than which nothing greater can be thought of), he was doing, in his way, exactly what Chapter 9 of this book did in a different way. He was explicating the notion we have of the supreme being and thus giving connotative significance to the word "God" as naming the supreme being.

Now consider the proposition "Wholes are greater than any of their parts." Being self-evident, the proposition is necessarily true. Accordingly, it is impossible in reality for wholes to be less than any of their parts. The necessary truth of the proposition renders an opposite state of affairs impossible.

A definite description of God includes "necessary existence" as a note in the notion thus being constructed. From the fact that we must include "necessary existence" in our notion of the supreme being, no consequences follow for any state of affairs in the real world.

If, instead, we had said that the proposition "God exists" is necessarily true, then the opposite state of affairs would have been impossible in the real world, as is the case with the necessary truth that wholes are greater than any of their parts.

To say that we must think of God as necessarily existing is not to assert that God exists or that God necessarily exists. A definite description cannot be interpreted as an existential assertion about God. It only tells us what meaning to give to the word "God" as the name of an object of thought.

Therefore, after we have formed a notion of God, one that includes thinking of God as having necessary existence (as incapable of not existing), it is in no way self-contradictory to ask whether that object of thought does or does not exist in reality.

Only those who persist in thinking that Anselm's argument has existential validity, which I have tried to show it does not have, will continue to maintain that, unlike every other existential proposition, the proposition "God exists" is both self-evident and necessarily true.

Since the proposition "God exists" is not meaningless (the significance of the word "God" having been established by our definite description); since the proposition is not self-contradictory or self-evidently false (there being nothing impossible about a reality which corresponds to that definite description); since we cannot, as pagans, know it to be true by direct acquaintance with the object in question; and since, as we have seen, it is not self-evidently true, only one possibility remains to be investigated.

Can a valid, cogent, and persuasive inference lead us to the conclusion that God exists, a conclusion we can affirm either beyond a reasonable doubt or by a preponderance of the evidence?

PART FOUR

Why the Best Traditional Argument Fails

CHAPTER 12

The Best Traditional Argument

THE PRECEDING CHAPTERS prepare us to consider the best traditional argument for the existence of God. It is sometimes miscalled "the cosmological argument," but it is often more correctly referred to as "the argument from contingency."

I have tried to refine the argument in order to make it conform to the requirements laid down in the chapters of Part Three—chapters that set the stage for attempts to argue for God's existence.

The argument will, therefore, avoid the error of begging the question of God's existence by assuming that the cosmos had a beginning—that at some past moment it was caused to come into existence out of nothing. It will also avoid the error of arguing to God as either first in a series of successive causes or first in a set of simultaneous co-acting causes.

As we have seen, to be valid, any existential inference must rest on at least one premise which is an existential proposition that can be affirmed as true. One of the best features of the argument to be considered is that the premise required is a proposition which asserts that you and I exist, the truth of which we will not question.

The proposition can, of course, be stated in a more general form, asserting the existence of all the finite, individual objects known by us to exist—all parts of the physical cosmos, from atoms and molecules to planets and stars. Nothing is gained by this generalization, if the existence of human beings (you and me) can be taken as representative of the existence of any other finite, individual thing known by us to exist.

It would seem that it can. If an inference to God's existence can be made from your existence and mine, it can also be made from the existence of any other finite, individual thing known by us to exist. The advantage of employing human individuals in the requisite existential premise is that their existence is most evident to us—most undeniable. At least my own is to me; and you would say the same about yours.

Another advantage is, perhaps, rhetorical rather than logical. Since the inference will not take the form of arguing that God exists as the *first* cause of an effect to be explained, God will be looked to as the one and only cause of that effect, acting directly and not through intermediaries. The effect to be explained, revealed by the existential premise in the argument, is the existence of human beings, your existence and mine. An argument which concludes that God is the direct cause of your existence and mine is one that has an appealing personal intimacy.

For the reasons just given, to which, perhaps, can be added the simplicity and elegance of the reasoning, the argument represents traditional thinking about God at its best. I will set it forth in three steps.

I will first explain the meaning of three crucial terms in the argument. I will then state and explain the five propositions that constitute the premises in the reasoning. Finally, I will carry that reasoning through to the conclusion which validly follows from the premises.

Let me caution the reader at once that the logical validity of the reasoning gives us no assurance that the conclusion reached by that reasoning is true in fact. Only if *all* the premises are themselves true will that be the case.

The Three Critical Terms

The three critical terms are (1) *contingent being*, (2) *necessary being*, and (3) *cause of being*.

The first two terms have no peculiar magic about them. They are simply verbal shortcuts which serve as substitutes for more precise but expanded phrasings of what is to be understood. Use of the more precise and expanded expressions in the statement of the argument would become tedious—both to reader and to author.

The explanation of the third term will involve our understanding of the distinction between a cause that causes being or existence, on the one hand, and a cause that causes becoming, or change and motion, on the other hand. Here it may be useful to substitute two Latin terms: *causa essendi* for "cause of being or existence" and *causa fieri* for "cause of becoming, change, or motion."

1. CONTINGENT BEING. I need only remind the reader of what has already been said in preceding chapters. That which exists, we said, either has its existence from, through, and in itself, or it has its existence from, through, and in another. A contingent being is any existent individual thing which has its existence from, through, and in another.

Another way of saying this is to say that its existence is dependent upon the existence and action of another; that its existence is conditioned by the existence and action of another, or of other things in the plural; and that its existence is caused by the action of another.

All this can be abbreviated to the statement that its existence is *ab alio*, the Latin word *alio* referring to the other from, through, and in which the individual existent in question has its existence. That would avoid raising the hackles that will be aroused in certain contemporary philosophical quarters by attaching the word "contingent" to the word "being" or "existence."

However, for most readers, who are happily unaware of the logical scruples of certain contemporary philosophers, using "contingent being" as the abbreviated expression will probably be more comfortable than using "existence *ab alio.*"

2. NECESSARY BEING. This is the other face of the matter, the other term in the distinction between that which exists *ab alio* (from, through, and in another), and that which exists *a se* (from, through, and in itself). That which exists *a se* or has *aseity* is a being that is independent, unconditioned, and uncaused.

According to the definite description which gives connotative significance to the word "God" as the name for the supreme being, God has *aseity*, which is strictly equivalent to saying that God is a *necessary being*, in the sense above.

Of the notes involved in our notion of God, it is more important, for the purposes of the argument, to say of the supreme being that its existence is uncaused, than to say that it is a being which cannot not exist. It would not be uncaused, of course, if instead of existing always, the supreme being came into being as contingent beings do.

3. CAUSE OF BEING (or *causa essendi*). To understand this term we must consider the contrasting term, expressed by the words "cause of becoming, change, or motion," or by "*causa fieri.*"

The billiard cue that sets a ball in motion, the food eaten by an animal organism that nourishes the animal and results in its growth, sunshine that bleaches the color out of a fabric, progenitors who produce progeny—all these represent efficient causes of (a) motions, (b) changes, such as increase in size or alteration in color, and (c) becoming, or what Aristotle called "generation," that is, the coming into existence of an individual that did not exist before.

The forgoing agents, including biological progenitors, do not act to cause the continuing existence of anything. Progenitors cause the becoming, or coming into existence, of progeny, but they can cease to be while the progeny continue to exist, and so if the continuing existence of the progeny needs a cause, the progenitors are *not* that cause.

Let me repeat that hypothetical statement: IF the continuing existence of the progeny needs a cause, then progenitors, who have ceased to exist while the progeny continue in existence, cannot be that cause. If we must look for such a cause, because it is needed, the cause we find will be a cause of existence (*causa essendi*), not a cause of becoming (*causa fieri*).

One more thing is needed to clarify the meaning of "cause of existence." It must be more than a necessary condition of the continuing existence of the object in question. It must be the efficient cause of that continuing existence.

I can give an example of what appears to be only a necessary condition, and not an efficient cause. Oxygen is a necessary condition for a candle flame to endure in an enclosed space after the candle has been lit. Remove the oxygen and the flame goes out. Oxygen is needed to support the continuing existence of the flame, even though it was a match, not oxygen, which caused the candle flame to come into existence in the first place. It would, therefore, appear that match and oxygen can be distinguished as cause of becoming and as a necessary condition of continuing existence.

From our everyday experience and from our scientific

knowledge of natural phenomena, I cannot give a single example of an efficient cause of existence that I am sure is an exnihilating cause—one that preserves the existence of something and prevents it from being *annihilated*, or from being reduced to absolute nothingness.

Let this much, then, suffice for the moment as preparation for the argument that follows.

The Five Premises in the Reasoning

Of the five, the first two are self-evident philosophical truths; the third and fourth are statements about contingent beings; and the fifth is the indispensable existential premise, asserting the existence of contingent beings.

1. THE EXISTENCE OF AN EFFECT THAT REQUIRES THE OPERATION OF A CO-EXISTENT CAUSE IMPLIES THE CO-EXISTENCE OF THAT CAUSE. What does not exist cannot operate or act. Hence, this proposition is no less self-evident than the more usual statement of the causal principle, which runs as follows: "The existence of an effect that requires the prior operation of a cause implies the prior existence as well as operation of that cause."

Not much more can be said about self-evident propositions such as these. Their truth will immediately be seen by those who understand what is being said. Very little can be done to remedy the deficient understanding on the part of those who do not immediately see the truth of such propositions.

2. WHATEVER EXISTS EITHER DOES OR DOES NOT NEED A CAUSE OF ITS EXISTENCE AT EVERY MOMENT OF ITS EXISTENCE; THAT IS, DURING THE TIME IN WHICH IT ENDURES, FROM THE MOMENT OF ITS COMING TO BE TO THE MOMENT OF ITS PASSING AWAY. The truth of this proposition rests on a set of ex-

clusive alternatives set up by the words "either does or does not." One of the two opposite states of affairs mentioned must be the case.

Only one point needs to be added to clarify what this proposition says. The cause needed is clearly a *cause of existence*, not a *cause of becoming*. That which needs a cause of existence is something that has already come into existence and not yet passed away. Whatever causes are responsible for its coming into existence, and for its passing away, we must still look for a cause of its continuing existence, IF and only IF that continuing existence does need a cause.

3. A CONTINGENT BEING IS ONE THAT NEEDS A CAUSE OF ITS CONTINUING EXISTENCE AT EVERY MOMENT OF ITS ENDURANCE IN EXISTENCE. What leads us to say this about contingent beings? It would appear to follow from the fact that their existence is *ab alio*, existence from, through, and in another. They do not have their existence from themselves. Therefore, if they continue to exist after they have been brought into being by a cause of their becoming, and if they do not have their existence from, through, and in themselves, we must look to some other for the cause of their existence.

Another way of seeing this is in the light of the principle of sufficient reason, stated as follows: Everything that exists or happens has a sufficient reason for existing or happening, either in itself or in another. Now, if contingent beings had their raison d'être in themselves, they would not be contingent; they would be necessary beings, beings *a se* or having aseity.

Existentialist philosophers who have become prominent in this century, particularly those who call themselves atheistic existentialists, confirm this insight in their talk about the absurdity of existence. Their angst, of which these existentialists make so much, arises from their conviction that individual human beings have no raison d'être whatsoever, neither in themselves nor in another. If they were right about that, their angst would, of course, be justified.

The reader should observe at once that the existentialist dogma violates the principle of sufficient reason. Waiving for the moment the truth or falsity of that dogma about the absurdity of existence, an important point remains to be noted. What does not have a raison d'être or a cause of its existence in itself, trembles on the verge of nothingness. Only if some cause exists and operates to preserve it in existence is it saved from annihilation, or being reduced to nothingness.

4. No CONTINGENT BEING CAUSES THE CONTINUING EXISTENCE OF ANY OTHER CONTINGENT BEING. This is *not* to say that contingent beings cannot cause the becoming, or coming into existence, of other contingent beings: for example, human parents procreating children, artists producing works of art. What *is* being said here can be summarized into two statements.

The first is thåt, in our ordinary experience and in our scientific knowledge of natural phenomena, we have no acquaintance with causal action on the part of natural causes that results in the continuing existence of anything. The causal action of natural causes results in motions, changes such as alterations in quality, increase or decrease in quantity, or generation and perishing, that is, coming to be and passing away.

Since all the natural causes we know are contingent things, it would appear to be the case that the causal action of contingent things does not result in the continuing existence of anything, but only in motions, changes, and generation or perishing.

The second statement calls attention to the fact that a contingent thing does not have its raison d'être, or the cause of its continuing existence, in itself, but in another. It would, therefore, appear reasonable to conclude that it cannot be the cause of the continuing existence of anything else.

5. CONTINGENT BEINGS EXIST IN THIS WORLD AND ENDURE, OR CONTINUE IN EXISTENCE, FROM THE MOMENT OF THEIR COMING TO BE TO THE MOMENT OF THEIR PASSING AWAY. The truth of this indispensable existential premise is vouchsafed for us by the incontrovertible knowledge that each of us has of his or her own existence and of our endurance from the moment of birth to the moment of death.

The Argument or Inference

In the light of the critical terms as clarified, and on the basis of the five premises as stated and explained, one is led to the conclusion that God, a necessary being, having existence *a se* (from, through, and in himself), exists and acts right now as the immediate or direct cause of the existence of you and me at this moment.

Stated another way, the conclusion reached is that there exists in reality a being which corresponds to the notion of the supreme being that we have formed—a being that always and necessarily exists and has an independent, unconditioned, and uncaused existence.

The reasoning involved can be summarized in a single, long paragraph, including a great many clauses, each beginning with IF and ending with a conclusion introduced by THEN. It runs as follows:

IF the existence of a certain effect implies the coexistence of its cause; and

IF whatever exists either does or does not need a cause of its continuing existence every moment of its existence; and

IF contingent beings are such that they do need a cause of their continuing existence at every moment of their existence; and

IF the cause they need must exist and act on them at every moment of their existence; and

IF no contingent being can be the cause that acts to sustain any
   other contingent being in existence; and

IF one or more contingent beings are known to exist, continuing in existence during the time that they endure;

THEN it follows that a necessary being exists as the cause which
   acts to sustain in existence the contingent beings that have
   a continuing existence while they endure.

One premise may be missing in the foregoing exposition of
the reasoning that constitutes an inference to the existence
of God. That missing premise has been presupposed.

Any object the existence of which we can think of must
be thought of as having its real existence either (1) necessarily or (2) contingently. It must be thought of as a being
that has its existence either (1) *a se* or (2) *ab alio*, either
(1) from, through, and in itself or (2) from, through, and in
another.

That being the case, IF no contingent being can supply
the causal action required to sustain in existence any other
contingent being, and IF every contingent being requires a
cause of its continuing existence, THEN we must look to a
necessary being as the cause we are searching for. If natural
causes do not explain what calls for explanation, we must
look to a supernatural cause.

The effect to be explained—the continuing existence of
contingent beings—justifies us, in accordance with Ockham's rule, in positing the existence in reality of an unobserved and unobservable hypothetical entity, the notion of
which we hold in mind by the theoretical construct we have
formed. That unobserved and unobservable hypothetical entity is the supreme being, or God.

This whole line of reasoning, with all its presuppositions,
can be encapsulated in a single short sentence: If contingent
beings exist, God exists; contingent beings do exist; therefore, God exists.

CHAPTER 13

The Faulty Premise

THE INFERENCE to the existence of God from the contingency of individual things is flawless in its reasoning. Affirming the truth of all the premises would lead us to affirm the truth of the conclusion, because it inexorably follows from those premises. If we knew the truth of the premises with certitude, the conclusion would be established with certitude. It might even be said to have been proved or demonstrated.

We need find only one premise questionable to make the conclusion questionable. One premise shown to be false would set the argument aside. It would not invalidate the argument logically, nor would it show that the conclusion, "God exists," is false. It would simply compel us to acknowledge that we had not succeeded in establishing that conclusion—that we had not supplied the grounds for a reasonable belief in the existence of the supreme being.

There is no difficulty with the first two propositions employed in the reasoning, for they state principles which are self-evidently true. Nor is there any difficulty with the last proposition, the fifth, which asserts your existence or mine. That cannot and will not be denied by you or me.

The fourth of the five propositions may require a little closer examination. It asserts that the individual things of this world, which have only a contingent existence, may cause other individual things to come into existence (parents generating offspring; artists producing works of art), but that they do not cause the continuing existence of the things they reproduce or produce.

The proposition, that contingent beings do not cause the continuing existence of anything, is confirmed by our common experience and our scientific knowledge of nature. When they operate as causes, the causal action of contingent beings results in motions, changes, or becomings—generation and corruption, or perishing. They are always and only *causa fieri*, never *causa essendi*.

Acknowledging the truth of the other four propositions, we are left with the third. There we run into trouble. That premise is faulty and, being untenable, it renders the reasoning inconclusive. Logically sound though it may be, it establishes nothing.

The third premise asserts that a contingent being needs an efficient cause of its continuing existence at every moment of its duration. The efficient cause of its becoming—its coming into existence—does not suffice. That merely gives it existence in the first place.

If the existence given it originally then belonged to it indefeasibly, so that it could not be annulled, it would never perish or pass away. Neither would it need an efficient cause of its continuing existence as long as it endured. But we know that it does not possess the existence given to it indefeasibly; its possession of existence can be annulled and it will perish or pass away.

While the individual exists, its existence may be supported by conditions necessary to maintain it, as the presence of oxygen is a condition necessary for the maintenance of a candle flame. It is a necessary, but not sufficient, condition; as such, it does not efficiently cause the continuing existence of the individual.

Let us grant that the existence which is conferred on an individual thing by the causes that produce or generate it (bring it into existence) is an existence which that thing does not possess indefeasibly. It will lose that existence when it ceases to be, and cease to be it will. That is precisely why we regard the individual's existence as contingent.

Nevertheless, we can still ask three questions: (1) Is it true that the individual, properly described as having contingent existence, needs an efficient cause of its existence at every moment while it endures? (2) Does the fact that the individual does not indefeasibly possess its existence afford us a sufficient reason for thinking that it needs an efficient cause of its continuing existence? (3) Is the individual's contingent existence a radical contingency or merely superficial?

It would be a radical contingency if it went to the very roots of the individual's being, with the consequence that, deprived of its existence, the individual would be reduced to nothingness or replaced by nothing. If, when it perishes, the individual is not reduced to nothingness, but is replaced by the same matter transformed into something else, then its contingency is superficial, not radical.

My answer to the first two questions is negative. To the third I reply by saying that the individual's contingency is superficial, not radical. Giving these three answers amounts to rejecting the third premise as false. Now let me state the reasons for my answers.

In the realm of motion, the modern discovery of the principle of inertia requires us to reject as false Aristotle's view that the continuing motion of a body set in motion needs a continuing efficient cause. According to Aristotle, the cue that hits the billiard ball merely initiates its motion. A column of air or something else must then keep pushing the ball to keep it in motion. It comes to rest either because a counteracting cause stops it, or because the efficient cause that is keeping it in motion while it continues to move, ceases to act on it.

This Aristotelian view prevailed for centuries, until Galileo and Newton discovered the principle of inertia, which states that a body set in motion (by an efficient cause) continues in motion in a straight line, and will do so indefinitely, until counteracting causes bring its movement to a halt or divert it in another direction.

The view held by mediaeval theologians, and some of their modern followers, concerning the continuing existence of contingent beings in the natural world, closely resembles the Aristotelian view concerning the continuing movement of a body set in motion.

As with local motion, a continuing efficient cause was thought to be needed for the body's continuing movement, so with regard to existence itself, a continuing efficient cause was thought to be needed for the individual's continuing existence.

I hold that something akin to the principle of inertia applies in the realm of existence, and leads us to reject the mediaeval view that the continuing existence of individual things needs the continuing action of an efficient cause.

Just as bodies set in motion continue in motion without the action of any efficient cause while they continue to move, and just as they come to rest only through the action of counteracting causes, so the individual things of nature, which are brought into existence by natural causes, continue in existence without the action of any efficient cause of their continuing existence; and their existence continues until the action of counteracting natural causes results in their perishing, or ceasing to be.

For the sake of illustration, let us consider the procreation of a living organism. Its biological progenitors, acting reproductively, are the efficient causes of its generation—its coming to be or having existence. While it endures, many natural conditions tend to sustain its life. They are necessary but not sufficient conditions of its continuing existence. Just as the body set in motion naturally tends to remain in motion (by inertia), so the organism brought into existence naturally tends to persevere in existence (by inertia).

Everything that exists has this natural tendency, not just living organisms, of which we often say that they have an instinct of self-preservation. What I am referring to goes deeper than that. It is the natural tendency of everything that exists to persevere in existence—by inertia, which is to say, without the action of an efficient cause that acts to cause its continuing existence.

Bodies continue in motion, once set in motion, until counteracting causes intervene to bring them to rest. Contingent individuals continue in existence, once given existence, until counteracting causes intervene to deprive them of their existence. Many different kinds of natural causes operate to destroy the life of an organism. The living organism survives until these causes operate efficaciously to produce its death.

The continuing existence of a contingent individual thing is, in part, *negatively* explained by the absence or inefficacy of counteracting causes—factors that, were they present and efficacious, would terminate the existence of the thing in question. It is also, in part, explained *positively* by the principle of inertia, extended from the physics of motion to the metaphysics of being.

This being so, and applying Ockham's rule, we have no need to posit the existence of a supernatural cause to explain what natural causes and natural tendencies suffice to explain.

I turn now to the answer I gave to the third question. There I mentioned that, while any individual thing which comes into existence and passes away is properly said to have a contingent existence, that contingency is only superficial, not radical. Understanding this point confirms the negative answers given to the first two questions.

Coming to be and ceasing to be in the physical world are not exnihilation and annihilation. What comes into existence by natural processes does not come into existence *out of nothing*. What passes out of existence does not pass *into nothingness;* it is not reduced to nothing.

The natural process of coming to be and passing away consists in a transformation of matter. Matter existing in one form or condition takes on existence in another form or condition. This particular individual is matter having a certain form. It came into existence by an alteration in the form or condition of prior existent matter; it passes out of existence by a similar alteration, when its matter persists in another form or condition.

The transformation—and disappearance—of this particular individual is the sign of its superficial, not its radical, contingency. The sign of its radical contingency would be its ceasing to be absolutely—*its annihilation, its reduction to nothingness, its replacement by nothing*.

In all our experience of the world and in all our scientific knowledge of nature, we have no evidence or indication of anything ever having been annihilated—or, for that matter, ever having been exnihilated. The natural process of generation and corruption, of coming to be and passing away, does not involve either exnihilation or annihilation.

The carpenter who takes wood and makes a chair brings that chair into existence by transforming the material he used for that purpose. When he takes the chair apart, in order to turn it into a stool or table, he may be said to destroy the chair, but not to annihilate it, for he has used the same material, the wood, and merely transformed it from being a chair into being a stool or a table.

The superficial contingency of the individual chair, which

the carpenter first made, lies in the fact that it does not have an indefeasible hold on its own individual existence. That its existence is not radically contingent is shown by the fact that, when it ceases to exist as that individual chair, it is not reduced to, or replaced by, nothingness, but rather by a stool or a table made out of the same matter. If instead of being transformed into another piece of furniture, the chair is consumed by fire, it turns into embers and ashes.

I am delighted that I have found some confirmation for my distinction between superficial and radical contingency in the writings of a devoted and penetrating disciple of Aquinas, Etienne Gilson. I have found it in those passages of Gilson's *Being and Some Philosophers* in which he acknowledges that natural generation and corruption—coming into being or passing away in the course of natural processes—are utterly different from exnihilation and annihilation, adding that the latter are never to be found in nature.

The confirmation I have found in Gilson, I cannot find in Aquinas, at least not explicitly. However, there is one statement in the *Summa Theologica* which has some bearing on the matter—the statement in which Aquinas asserts that God annihilates nothing.

A moment's further reflection enables us to draw a significant insight from that statement. Let us suppose that the third premise had been true instead of false. We would then have to affirm that you and I are sustained in existence by the supernatural action of God as the indispensable efficient cause of our continuing to exist. Accordingly, when we die, God would be directly responsible for our death, by ceasing to act as the needed efficient cause of our continuing existence.

Truly religious persons, who believe that everything which happens is within the ordination of Divine providence, do not—or, at least, should not—blame God for the death of loved ones. Death comes about through natural causes. It is simply the perishing of a particular individual and not his total annihilation.

While the individuality of a particular person, or of some particular thing, may disappear with that person's death or that thing's destruction through natural processes, everything else remains. Nothing is annihilated.

This philosophical truth may give cold comfort to the bereaved, who have lost something of value to them, but the truth is unaffected by that fact.

PART FIVE

From the Cosmos to God

CHAPTER 14

A Truly Cosmological Argument

THE ARGUMENT from the contingent existence of individual things that are parts of the cosmos is not an argument which can truly be called "cosmological." That epithet rightly belongs to an argument in which the effect to be explained is the existence of the cosmos as a whole.

Stated in the briefest possible fashion, a truly cosmological argument runs as follows: IF the existence of the cosmos as a whole needs to be explained, and IF it cannot be explained by natural causes, THEN we must look to the existence and action of a supernatural cause for its explanation.

Once again, it is necessary to remind the reader that we began this inquiry by assuming that the cosmos always existed. We made this assumption in order to avoid begging the question of God's existence. However, we can still ask whether the uncreated cosmos needs a cause of its everlasting, continuing existence.

We have already seen, in the preceding chapter, that the individual things which are parts of the cosmos do not need a supernatural cause of their continuing existence. Natural causes and the principle of inertia in being suffice to explain that. Why, then, should we think it is an open question whether the cosmos as a whole needs a supernatural cause of its continuing existence?

The answer rests on a distinction introduced in the preceding chapter—the distinction between superficial and radical contingency. We saw there that the existence of individual things is only superficially contingent. If anything is radically contingent, it must be the cosmos as a whole, and that fact opens the door to considering whether the cosmos needs a supernatural cause to sustain it in existence.

To say that the existence of the cosmos is radically contingent is to say that its ceasing to be would not consist in its transmutation into another cosmos, but would consist, instead, in its replacement by absolutely nothing.

If that were so, the cause needed to sustain it in existence would act to prevent it from being reduced to nothingness. It would be an exnihilating cause that is preservative in its action, whereas if an exnihilating cause initially brought the cosmos into existence, it would be creative in its action.

Exnihilation, in short, can be either creative or preservative; but in either case, exnihilation involves the action of a supernatural cause. No natural cause exnihilates anything, either creatively or preservatively.

Before I state the four propositions that constitute the premises of a truly cosmological argument, it may be useful to consider the similarities and differences between the cosmos and the individual things that are its parts or components.

The most important difference is that the cosmos as a

whole is in no sense an individual thing. It may be a unique singular object of thought, for, as the totality of everything that exists physically, there can be only one cosmos at a given time. However, that totality, comprising as it does all the individual things that exist physically, is not itself an individual thing, as a single electron, atom, or molecule is, as a single living organism is, or as a single celestial body is.

Like the solar system in which we live, or like the galaxy which is the home of our solar system, the cosmos as a whole is an assemblage (unthinkably vast) of individual things. The total aggregation appears to have something like an organized or systematic structure, but it also appears not to be a monolithic organization or system of everything that exists physically.

When we think of the highly organized and systematic structure of the human organism, the difference between its structure and that of the cosmos should prevent us from regarding it as the microcosm which is nothing but a smaller version of the macrocosm.

Much that happens in the cosmos appears to happen by chance. The cosmos manifests disorder as well as order. While the cosmos is, by its very name, the opposite of pure chaos, it is not without that element of randomness which, carried to the extreme, would result in chaos.

Another difference between the cosmos and its individual parts or components lies in the fact that the latter, with the possible exception of electrons and protons, come into existence, endure for a time, and pass away, not into nothing, but by transformation into something else. If the cosmos were to come into being and pass away, it would come into being out of nothing, and pass away by reduction to nothingness. This is our reason for saying that, IF the existence of the cosmos is contingent, its contingency, unlike that of individual things, is radical, not superficial.

Still another difference is that, while each individual physical thing is a part of the cosmos, the cosmos as the totality of all such components is not a part of any larger physical whole. As parts of the cosmos, individual things are dependent for their continuing existence upon the continuing existence of the cosmos as a whole. Were it reduced to nothingness, they also would cease to exist.

The continuing existence of the cosmos is a necessary, though perhaps not the sufficient, condition of the continuing existence of its component parts, since the inertia of being also plays a role in their continuing existence. We can say, therefore, that the continuing existence of individual things is dependent and conditioned, but uncaused, that is, uncaused in the sense that it does not need the action of an efficient cause.

When we turn from individual things that are parts of the cosmos, to the cosmos as a whole, we must speak in a contrary vein. Its continuing existence is independent and unconditioned, since the cosmos as a whole does not exist as a part of any larger whole. *But is it uncaused? Does it need the action of an efficient cause to sustain it in existence?* That is still a question to be answered.

Against the background of all these differences between the cosmos and individual things, let us now consider the respects in which they are similar.

For one thing, both are physical. When we speak of the realm of nature, we are referring to both.

Both are observable, either directly by aided or unaided perception, or indirectly by instrumentation and pointer readings. The statement that the cosmos is observable must be qualified by saying that, in its vast reaches, parts of the cosmos may lie forever beyond our power to observe or even detect. Technologically insuperable barriers may forever prevent us from penetrating the veil that separates us from parts of the cosmos that once existed backward in time, or that now exist outward in space.

Nevertheless, to say that everything which is part of the spatiotemporal existence of the cosmos as a whole cannot be observed by us is not to say that the cosmos is not observable at all. We should say, perhaps, that while individual things may be *completely* observable, the cosmos as a whole is only *partially* observable.

Another similarity between the cosmos as a whole and its individual components is that both are mutable—forever undergoing change, whether that change is in place, in quality, or in quantity. Still one other similarity between the cosmos and some of its component parts, such as subatomic particles and black holes, lies in the fact that they are not objects of thought by means of empirically formed concepts (concepts arising from perceptual experience). Instead, they are objects of thought by means of theoretical constructs.

In this last respect, the cosmos as a whole and some of its aforementioned components are like the supreme being as an object of thought. Considering the cosmos as a whole, and not its components parts, we can also say that, as objects of thought, neither it nor the supreme being is thought of as part of anything else; neither is thought of as coming into existence and passing away; neither is thought of as having a dependent or conditioned existence.

There the similarities stop, and differences begin. We think of the cosmos as physical, material, mutable, and observable (directly or indirectly), whereas we have found that we must think of the supreme being as non-physical, immaterial, immutable, and totally unobservable by us.

Above all, we do not have to ask whether the cosmos exists. We know that it does. But we cannot avoid asking whether God exists, and seeking the answer to that question.

In addition, we have found that we must think of God as having an uncaused existence, and, because of God's aseity, also an independent and unconditioned existence. If we can find reasonable grounds for believing in the existence of the supreme being, we do not have to ask whether God's existence is uncaused.

Knowing that the cosmos exists, we do not know whether its existence is uncaused. We must ask concerning the cosmos, as we do not have to ask concerning God (IF God exists), whether its existence is caused or uncaused.

Here, then, to sum it up, is the striking difference between the cosmos and God as objects of thought. We know that the cosmos exists, but we must ask whether its existence is caused or uncaused—whether it has a necessary or a radically contingent existence. We do not know whether the supreme being exists, but, IF God does exist, we do not have to ask whether God's existence is caused or uncaused—whether God has necessary or radically contingent existence.

A point that may have escaped notice should also be stressed. When we say that the cosmos has an independent and unconditioned existence, we are using the words "independent" and "unconditioned" to signify that the cosmos does not depend for its existence upon a larger whole to which it belongs, as its own parts do; and that its existence is not conditioned by factors outside itself, as the existence of individual things is conditioned by factors operating in their cosmic environment.

I am now prepared to state the propositions that constitute a cosmological argument for God's existence. Only four propositions are needed as premises. They are as follows:

1. THE EXISTENCE OF AN EFFECT REQUIRING THE CONCURRENT EXISTENCE AND ACTION OF AN EFFICIENT CAUSE IMPLIES THE EXISTENCE AND ACTION OF THAT CAUSE. The causal principle, thus stated, is self-evidently true, as has been said before.

2. THE COSMOS AS A WHOLE EXISTS. Here we have the existential assertion that is indispensable as a premise in any

existential inference. While it does not have the same certitude possessed by my assertion of my own existence, or your assertion of yours, it can certainly be affirmed beyond a reasonable doubt.

3. THE EXISTENCE OF THE COSMOS AS A WHOLE IS RADICALLY CONTINGENT, WHICH IS TO SAY THAT, WHILE NOT NEEDING AN EFFICIENT CAUSE OF ITS COMING TO BE, SINCE IT IS EVERLASTING, IT NEVERTHELESS DOES NEED AN EFFICIENT CAUSE OF ITS CONTINUING EXISTENCE, TO PRESERVE IT IN BEING AND PREVENT IT FROM BEING REPLACED BY NOTHINGNESS. In the light of all that has gone before, there should be no difficulty in understanding what this proposition says. The only question is whether it is true. I will return to that question presently.

4. *If* THE COSMOS NEEDS AN EFFICIENT CAUSE OF ITS CONTINUING EXISTENCE TO PREVENT ITS ANNIHILATION, *Then* THAT CAUSE MUST BE A SUPERNATURAL BEING, SUPERNATURAL IN ITS ACTION, AND ONE THE EXISTENCE OF WHICH IS UNCAUSED; IN OTHER WORDS, THE SUPREME BEING, OR GOD. We have understood that no natural cause can be an exnihilating cause, and that no natural cause is uncaused in its existence or action. In the light of this understanding, we are in a position to affirm the truth of this hypothetical proposition—this IF-THEN premise. Since *natural* and *supernatural* represent an exhaustive set of alternatives, the cause being sought must be supernatural if it cannot be natural.

Two of the four premises—the first and last—appear to be true with certitude. The second is true beyond a reasonable doubt. If the one remaining premise—the third—is also true beyond a reasonable doubt, we can conclude, beyond a reasonable doubt, that God exists and acts to sustain the cosmos in existence.

The one remaining question, to be considered in the next

chapter, is whether that third premise is true—beyond a reasonable doubt, or even by a preponderance of reasons in favor of affirming it, as against reasons in favor of denying it.

In the argument from contingency, set forth in Chapter 12, there was one premise that we subsequently found, in Chapter 13, to be not only faulty, but false. I hope to be able to show, in Chapter 15, that the one premise in the cosmological argument that remains questionable is neither faulty nor false, but true.

If I succeed in doing that, then the cosmological argument will be seen to be not only flawless reasoning, but also reasoning that provides us with reasonable grounds for belief in God. Persuaded of this, the reader may have only one complaint left.

The argument may leave the reader cold because, unlike the unsuccessful argument from contingency, God's causal action does not touch him or her directly, but only indirectly as a part of the cosmos.

· This and other dissatisfactions with a purely philosophical inquiry concerning God's existence, even when carried to successful completion, I will consider in Chapter 17.

CHAPTER 15

One Remaining Question

THAT QUESTION is whether the cosmos as a whole is radically contingent—whether it is true that the cosmos needs a supernatural cause that acts to exnihilate it by preserving it in existence and prevent it from being reduced to nothingness.

The question can be stated in another way. Is it possible for the cosmos that now exists to cease to exist and be replaced by nothing at all?

In the argument from the contingent existence of the individual things that are parts of the cosmos, we took as a sign of their contingency that they come into existence and pass away, enduring only for a limited period of time. In that case, however, their coming into existence was not a coming to be out of nothing, nor was their ceasing to exist a reduction to nothingness.

Seeing that the contingency of their existence was only superficial, not radical, we also saw that the principle of inertia of being, together with other natural factors supportive of their existence, sufficed to explain their continuing existence.

But when we consider the cosmos, we cannot employ coming into existence and passing away as a sign of its contingent existence, since we have assumed that the cosmos exists everlastingly. What, then, can we resort to as the sign of the contingency—and the radical contingency at that—of the cosmos as a whole?

One argument that has been used by many traditional theologians, both mediaeval and modern, must be dismissed as fallacious. It asserts that, since all the parts or components of the cosmos are contingent in existence, the whole, therefore, must be contingent in existence, too.

The error here is twofold. In the first place, if we accept what nuclear physics teaches us—that electrons and protons, the building blocks of the cosmos, as it were, cannot cease to exist once they do exist—then at least some of the components of the cosmos do not perish by being transformed into something else. Hence we cannot say that the cosmos as a whole is contingent in existence, because all of its components are contingent in existence.

In the second place, even if all its components were contingent in existence, it would still be fallacious to say that the cosmos as a whole is contingent in existence. The fallacy committed is traditionally called "the fallacy of composition"—of arguing from a characteristic of all the parts of a whole to a characterization of the whole.

Sometimes we can validly make such an inference as, for example, when we say that a community of human beings is wealthy because all of its individual members are wealthy. "Being wealthy" is the kind of characteristic that is properly predicable of both parts and whole, and so the inference from parts to whole is legitimate.

However, when the characteristic in question is not properly predicable of both parts and whole, the inference is illegitimate or fallacious. From the fact that every member of the human race has a mother, we cannot infer that the human race as a whole has a mother. "Having a mother" is predicable of individual human beings, but not of the human race as a whole.

It would appear that "contingent existence" is properly predicable of the individual things that are components of the cosmos and also of the cosmos as a whole. Now, then, an inference from a characteristic of parts to a characterization of the whole is legitimate only if two conditions are fulfilled. First, the characteristic in question must be predicable of all the parts, not just of some; second, it must not only be properly predicable of both parts and whole, but it must also be predicable *in exactly the same sense of both*, not in different senses.

The contingency of the cosmos as a whole (IF it is contingent) must, as we have seen, be radical, not superficial, whereas the contingency of individual things is superficial, not radical. Hence, we cannot infer the contingency of the cosmos as a whole from the contingency of its parts, even if all the parts, including electrons and protons, were contingent in their existence, as indicated by their coming into existence and passing away.

So far we have not been able to find grounds for thinking that the cosmos as a whole is contingent in its existence— radically contingent in that if it ceased to exist it would not be transformed into something else but would be replaced by nothingness.

Should we be unable to affirm the radical contingency of the cosmos, we would then have no grounds for thinking that the cosmos as a whole needs a supernatural cause to sustain it in existence. Complying with Ockham's rule governing inferences to the existence of unobservable hypothetical entities, we would then not be justified in positing the existence of God as the supernatural cause needed to explain the continuing existence of a radically contingent cosmos.

Our appeal to the principle of inertia in being made it unnecessary for us to posit God as the efficient cause of the continuing existence of the physical things that are parts of the cosmos. It sufficed to explain their perseverance in being from the moment that they came into existence until the moment that counteracting causes brought their existence to an end. Perhaps the principle of inertia might similarly suffice to explain the perseverance in being of the cosmos as a whole, even if it is radically contingent in its existence.

The physical principle of inertia—the inertia that is the property of bodies in motion—applies to bodies that have been set in motion. When they are set in motion, they continue in motion by inertia until counteracting causes terminate their motion and bring them to rest.

The principle of inertia also applies to bodies at rest. They remain indefinitely at rest until some influence acting on them sets them in motion. They are, in other words, inert until caused to move.

It would thus appear to be the case that the principle of inertia is applicable to the maintenance or continuation of a certain state (either being at rest or being in motion), not to change of state (from being at rest to being in motion, or from being in motion to being at rest).

Let us now turn from bodies in motion or at rest, and from the physical principle of inertia, to its metaphysical counterpart, which is applicable to existence and non-existence.

Inertia of being might explain the continuing existence of

the cosmos IF the cosmos were initially brought into existence by God as its creator. This would parallel the explanation of the continuing existence of progeny after they are initially brought into existence by their progenitors. In both cases, the action of an efficient cause accounts for the change of state, and inertia for the continuation in that state.

However, this employment of the principle of inertia as applicable to the continuing existence of the cosmos rests upon a hypothesis—the IF clause which reads: IF the cosmos were initially brought into existence by its creator. On this hypothesis there may be no need to posit the existence of God as preserver of the cosmos. However, we cannot fail to note that the hypothesis does posit the existence of God as its creator.

Let us persist in our rejection of this hypothesis and return to our initial assumption of an uncreated cosmos. On that assumption, we must renew our effort to find a reason for thinking that the continuing existence of the cosmos needs an efficient cause for its perpetuation in that state.

That reason is to be found in the fact that the cosmos which now exists is only one of many possible universes that might have existed in the infinite past, and that might still exist in the infinite future.

This is not to say that any cosmos other than this one ever did exist in the past, or ever will exist in the future. It is not necessary to go that far in order to say that other universes might have existed in the past and might exist in the future.

If other universes are possible, then this one also is merely possible, not necessary—not the only cosmos that can ever exist in an infinite extent of time.

How do we know that the present cosmos is only a possible universe (one of many possibilities that might exist), not a necessary universe (the only one that can ever exist)?

We can infer it from the fact that the arrangement and disarray—the order and disorder—of the present cosmos might have been otherwise, might have been different from what it is. There is no compelling reason to think that the natural laws which govern the present cosmos are the only possible natural laws. The cosmos as we know it manifests chance and random happenings, as well as lawful behavior. Even the electrons and protons, which are thought to be imperishable once they exist as the building blocks of the present cosmos, might not be the building blocks of a different cosmos.

The next step in the argument is the crucial one. It consists in saying that whatever might have been otherwise in shape or structure is something that also might not exist at all.

That which *cannot* be otherwise also *cannot* not exist; and conversely, what necessarily exists cannot be otherwise than it is. The truth that is the thin thread on which the cosmological argument hangs runs parallel to the truth just stated. Whatever can be otherwise than it is can also simply not be at all. A cosmos which can *be otherwise* is one that also can *not be;* and conversely, a cosmos that is capable of not existing at all is one that can be otherwise than it now is.

Applying this insight to the fact that the existing cosmos is merely one of a plurality of possible universes, we come to the conclusion that the cosmos, radically contingent in existence, would not exist at all were its existence not caused.

A merely possible cosmos cannot be an uncaused cosmos. A cosmos that is radically contingent in its existence, and needs a cause of that existence, needs a supernatural cause—one that exists and acts to exnihilate this merely possible cosmos, thus preventing the realization of what is always possible for a merely possible cosmos; namely, its absolute non-existence or reduction to nothingness.

The cosmological argument, carried out in this way, appears to establish the existence of the supreme being that acts as the exnihilating cause of this merely possible cosmos, and so explains why it continues to exist. The reasoning conforms to Ockham's rule. We have found it necessary to posit the existence of God, the supreme being, in order to explain what needs to be explained—the actual existence here and now of a merely possible cosmos.

We observed at the very beginning of this inquiry that two assumptions about the cosmos are equally tenable. Reason is unable to show that we must adopt one rather than the other. However, in an inquiry concerning God's existence, we found it necessary to assume that the cosmos has always existed. To assume that it initially came into existence out of nothing would require us to posit God's existence as the cause of its creation.

We would then, in effect, beg the very question under investigation. The conclusion to be established is implicitly contained in that assumption, for if the cosmos was created, there had to be a cause of its creation. We, therefore, had to make the opposite assumption—that the cosmos was uncreated or, in other words, that the cosmos never came into existence out of nothing.

The cosmological argument has now brought us to the conclusion that God exists not as the creative, but as the preservative cause of the continuing actual existence of a possible cosmos. This means that we have reached the conclusion at which our inquiry aimed. It also means that we would no longer be begging the question about God's existence if we now entertained the assumption that we rejected at the beginning of this inquiry. Let us, therefore, consider what follows from assuming that this possible cosmos, now actual, has not always existed, but at some past moment came into existence out of nothing.

On that assumption, we have a second form of the cosmological argument. The first form, based on the assumption of the everlasting existence of the cosmos, gives us reason for believing in the existence of God as the *preservative* cause of the continuing existence of the cosmos. The second form gives us reason for believing in the existence of God as the *creative* cause of the initial coming into existence of the cosmos.

To bring into existence out of nothing that which, without such creative action, would not exist is to exnihilate. To preserve in existence that which, without such preservative action, would cease to exist and be reduced to nothingness is also to exnihilate. Neither form of exnihilating action is within the power of natural causes. Hence we are led to conclude that a supernatural cause exists to accomplish either result.

We must never forget that we cannot resort to the second form of the cosmological argument until the first form of that argument persuades us that we have sufficient reason to affirm God's existence. Once we affirm God's existence on the assumption of an uncreated cosmos, we can turn to the more likely assumption of a created cosmos. That a possible cosmos has everlastingly existed is less likely than the opposite.

I wish, in concluding this chapter, to note one consequence of the difference between these two forms of a truly cosmological argument for God's existence—one based on the fact that an exnihilating *preservative* cause is needed to explain the continuing existence in actuality of a merely possible cosmos; the other based on the fact that an exnihilating *creative* cause is needed to explain the actualization of a merely possible cosmos.

In the latter case, the creative action of the supernatural cause produces the cosmos as a whole, which means that it produces the natural causes which, in their ongoing operation, account for the development of the cosmos since its initiation.

In the former case, the preservative action of the supernatural cause sustains in existence the cosmos as whole, and thereby sustains the operation of all the natural causes at work from moment to moment.

That preservative action can also be interpreted as sustaining the existence of all the individual things that are parts of the cosmos and that, being perishable, are superficially contingent in their existence.

This includes you and me. We would cease to exist at this very moment if the cosmos as a whole ceased to exist, the possibility of which is prevented from happening by the exnihilating *preservative* action of God.

CHAPTER 16

How Credible Is the Conclusion
We Have Reached?

RATIONAL PHILOSOPHICAL INQUIRY is a persistent effort to explain what needs to be explained and cannot be explained by scientific investigation, or any other form of inquiry that employs as its means perceptual observations and reflective or analytical thought.

Rational philosophical inquiry comes to a halt only when there is nothing left to be explained, or when the explanation must appeal to something that is in itself inexplicable. The explanation of the actual existence of a merely possible cosmos appeals to something that may appear to be inexplicable—an uncaused cause; but since that uncaused cause is the supreme being, having aseity, it has in itself a sufficient reason for its own existence.

On the other hand, one might say that the existence of the cosmos is itself inexplicable because its existence is uncaused.

In that case, everything which happens in the cosmos might be explained by reference to the operation of natural causes, but the existence of the cosmos itself would remain inexplicable, because a merely possible cosmos does not have in itself a sufficient reason for its own existence.

Why should there be something rather than nothing? Any attempt to answer this question will confront the mystery of that which we cannot fully understand or explain. In any case, we appear to be confronted with an ultimate option, an ultimate choice between (a) looking upon the cosmos as an actualized possibility that is explained by reference to Divine causal action, or (b) taking the cosmos itself to be inexplicable because it exists without being caused.

What determines our choice between these alternatives? It depends entirely on where we stand on the question whether the cosmos is or is not an actualized possibility, one out of a plurality of possible universes.

If we are persuaded that it is a merely possible universe, then we are also persuaded that its existence is radically contingent and that it requires an exnihilating cause, either for its creation out of nothing (the actualization of its possibility) or for the preservation of its continuing existence and the prevention of its being reduced to nothing, or both.

I have used the word "persuaded" rather than "convinced" for the following reason. On the initial assumption we had to make, in order not to beg the question of God's existence, we had to try to establish the existence of the supreme being as the exnihilating preservative—not creative—cause of the universe's everlasting existence.

In that effort, the crucial premise—the proposition that the cosmos is radically contingent and needs an efficient cause of its continuing existence—cannot be affirmed with certitude, but only beyond a reasonable doubt.

Having accomplished that, we are then in a position to consider the alternative assumption, which is equally tenable;

namely, that the cosmos has not always existed, but initially came into existence out of nothing. On that assumption, the proposition "God exists" can be established with certitude, for it is impossible that something should come into existence out of nothing without the action of an exnihilating creative cause. But, since we cannot make that alternative assumption until we have first found reason to believe in God, on the basis of our initial assumption of an everlasting cosmos, our conclusion that God exists cannot be affirmed with certitude, but only beyond a reasonable doubt.

If that, in the eyes of some readers, sets too high a standard of probative force for the reasoning by which we have reached the conclusion, I am quite willing to settle for less. If I am able to say no more than that a preponderance of reasons favor believing that God exists, I can still say I have advanced reasonable grounds for that belief.

The conclusion that God exists has not been proved or demonstrated. Nothing that has been said should result in conviction with certitude.

I, for one, am left with something less than that, but something that is, in my judgment, more desirable than its opposite. I am persuaded that God exists, either beyond a reasonable doubt or by a preponderance of reasons in favor of that conclusion over reasons against it. I am, therefore, willing to terminate this inquiry with the statement that I have reasonable grounds for affirming God's existence.

Each reader must decide for himself whether or not he is willing to make a statement to the same effect.

PART SIX

Epilogue:
The Chasm
and the Bridge

CHAPTER 17

To the Chasm's Edge

IF WE ARE PERSUADED that the physical cosmos is not the ultimate, inexplicable, and uncaused reality, then we are under a rational obligation to posit the existence of the supreme being as the supernatural—and uncaused—cause that explains the preservation of the cosmos if its existence is everlasting, or its creation if it came into being out of nothing.

We discharge that rational obligation when we affirm God's existence—when we acknowledge that we have reasonable grounds for believing in God, not with certitude, but beyond a reasonable doubt.

In discharging this obligation, natural theology reaches a limit beyond which rational philosophical inquiry cannot go. Unlike sacred theology, it does *not* begin with arguments for God's existence and then proceed to consider the nature of God, the creation of the cosmos, the special place of human persons in the cosmos, the relation of man and all other creatures to God, the law and the grace that God gives to human beings for their guidance and assistance, the immortality of the human soul and the afterlife, sin and salvation, Divine rewards and punishments, Divine providence and Divine government.

These and many other subjects that are treated in sacred theology can have no place in natural theology or philosophical inquiry. They lie beyond the power of reason to consider when rational inquiry is conducted in a pagan context and is, therefore, totally unilluminated and undirected by religious faith.

As compared with the thickness of sacred theology, natural theology is very, very thin. As the late William Temple, archbishop of York, said, it "ends in a hunger which it cannot satisfy." Its closing words are those of Augustine in the tenth book of his *Confessions* when, asking "the whole frame of the world about God," he received the answer: "I am not He, but He made me."

Purely philosophical theology begins with the consideration of all the prerequisites of a cautious and critical inquiry concerning God's existence, and terminates with a cautious and critical appraisal of how far it can go in providing reasonable grounds for belief in God. It can go no further. It carries us up to the edge of the chasm that separates what Pascal called "the God of the philosophers" from "the God of Abraham, Isaac, and Jacob," and of Moses, Jesus, and Mohammed.

Pascal himself turned his back on the God of the philosophers and, extraordinary intellect and scientific genius that he was, crossed to the other side of the chasm not by reason, but by a leap of faith.

If Pascal was right, if reason cannot build a bridge across the chasm, however fragile and shaky that bridge may be, then readers may be justified in putting this book down with a deep sense of dissatisfaction—Pascal's dissatisfaction with the God of the philosophers. The God of the philosophers is not an object of worship, not a source of guidance and help to human beings in their trials and tribulations, not the supreme being one prays to. The eminent Spanish philosopher José Ortega y Gasset has pointed out that there is a world of difference between *believing that God exists* and *believing in God*—confiding in him and having hope in him.

Granted that the reasoning carried on in this book is an interesting philosophical exercise. Granted that it may result in some change of mind on the part of some pagans who thought they had no grounds for believing that God exists. Granted even that it makes the universe in which we live more intelligible by explaining its existence, which would value does that have? How does that change the meaning of human life, or the course of our lives?

otherwise be inexplicable and absurd, as contemporary existentialists would have it. What of it? What practical use or

In my view, a philosopher cannot avoid such questions, or shrug them off. Nor should a philosopher be content to tell those who ask questions of this sort: "Go and do as Pascal did. Turn your back on the God of the philosophers and take a leap of faith across the chasm; for, on the other side, you will find the God you are looking for, who will make a difference to the meaning of life for you and to the course of your own life."

The philosopher can do a little more than that. He can build a bridge to the other side of the chasm by attempting to show—by reason and reason alone—the affinity that exists between the God of the philosophers and the God of the worship.

faithful, as objects of thought. That he can do, but no more, and that still remains insufficient for religious belief and

Religious belief in and worship of the God on the other

side of the chasm draws its vigor and vitality from an article
of religious faith that lies beyond the power of reason to do
more than discuss. That article of faith is belief in the immortality of the human soul and the promise of life hereafter.

Philosophical reflection can appraise all the scientific evidence and the facts of common experience that have a bearing on the special status of man in the order of nature. It
can establish, beyond a reasonable doubt, the conclusion that
man differs in kind from all other animals, by virtue of having intellectual powers and powers of action not possessed
by them to any degree. It can explain why a human being,
and nothing else on earth, is properly regarded as a person.
To this extent, philosophy makes contact with the Western
religious belief that man and man alone is made in the image
of God, who is also a person, not a thing.

I think I have done this much in a book that I wrote some
years ago, entitled *The Difference of Man and the Difference It Makes*. But, beyond this, philosophy cannot go. Belief in the immortality of the human soul, in its separate
existence apart from the body after the death of the organism, in its having a personal life hereafter, and in its re-
union with a resurrected body at the end of the world—all
this lies beyond reason's power to establish, even by a preponderance of the evidence, much less beyond reasonable
doubt.

Putting aside these additional considerations that lie at the
heart of religious faith and worship, there is still some point
and value in pushing rational inquiry as far as it can go to
bridge the chasm between the God of the philosophers and
the God of religious faith, either as objects of thought or as
realities, the existence of which may be believed.

Before I undertake to do that in the following chapter,
let me call attention to one of the most important differences
between the two objects of thought. The definite description that conferred connotative significance on the word

"God," for the purposes of philosophical inquiry, omitted entirely any consideration of the moral goodness of the supreme being, the justice and mercy of God, or His loving benevolence toward creatures.

We had no grounds for adding these notes to our notion of God as the supreme being—one which we must think of as really existing and as necessarily existing. There is no rational necessity to think of the supreme being as morally good, as just and merciful, or as benevolently disposed toward the world of men.

Precisely because purely philosophical theology is obliged to abstain from such considerations, it is also exempt from the atheist's attacks. Those attacks are never directed against the God of the philosophers, but against the God of religious faith. They are rooted in the apparent conflict between the moral goodness, justice, mercy, and benevolence attributed to God by religious faith, and the existence of both physical and moral evil in the world.

Such attacks also make much of the incompatibility between God's omnipotence and omniscience, and man's possession of freedom of choice between good and evil and moral responsibility for making the wrong choice. They deny that God's ways, however inscrutable, can ever be justified to man, as theodicy (which is an appendage of sacred theology) attempts to do.

I mention this in order to warn those who, having come this far, may be tempted to step gingerly onto the fragile bridge that philosophy can build across the chasm. On the other side of the bridge stand not only religious theists, but also anti-religious atheists. If those who venture onto the bridge should subsequently, through faith, join the community of the former, they must be prepared to encounter and respond to the serious questions raised by the latter.

As I have tried to explain as clearly as possible, neither the consummation nor the confrontation will occur through the exercise of reason alone. There are no anti-philosophical atheists, only anti-religious ones.

Reason can build a bridge, but it cannot carry anyone across to the other side. Pascal's leap of faith across an un-bridged chasm may not be necessary, but the encouragement and attraction of faith are needed to motivate using the bridge to make the crossing.

CHAPTER 18

Bridging the Chasm

THE BRIDGE that philosophical thought can throw across the chasm is hardly the kind that is supported by sturdy foundations sunk in solid rock. It is rather like a rope bridge that hangs suspended from anchorages fastened somewhat insecurely on opposite sides.

Two things make it possible to fasten the ropes that run from one side to the other. One is a set of notes than can be excogitated out of the notion we have already formed of God as the supreme being. These notes, not mentioned before, name attributes of the deity who is worshiped in the three monotheistic religions of the West. They were not mentioned before simply because they would have played no role in our inquiry concerning God's existence.

The other tie-in consists of considerations that do not derive from the notion we formed of the supreme being in order to inquire about God's existence. Instead, they can be developed by thought from the reasons we have given for positing the existence of the supreme being in order to explain the existence of the cosmos. These considerations also tie in with attributes ascribed to God by persons of religious faith.

I will first attempt to show how thought excogitates the first set of notes mentioned above. I will then turn to the second set of considerations. Of the two, the second carries less weight than the first; its supporting ropes being unequal in strength, the bridge is a trifle unbalanced.

If I cannot think of God except as the supreme being, must I not also think of God as omnipotent? If the notion of God does not include the note of omnipotence, that allows a more powerful being to be thought of. This would contradict our original notion which claimed to present an object of thought than which no greater can be thought of.

It would seem to follow, therefore, that "supreme being" and "omnipotent being" are inseparable notes in our thinking about God. As the word plainly indicates, an omnipotent being lacks no power. It has the power to do whatever can be done, and is subject to no power outside itself or greater than itself.

Unlike such notes as "infinite," "immutable," "immaterial," "unconditioned," or "uncaused"—all of which are negative in their significance—"omnipotent" is positive. We understand these negative notes simply by negating what is signified by the same words unnegated. We do understand what it means to say that something is mutable, material, or caused; and when we say that two or more things are mutable, material, or caused, we are saying that they are univocally alike in these respects. They are mutable, material, or caused in the same sense of these words.

When we say that God is immaterial, we are saying that God is *not* material in that sense of the word which is applicable to all material things. That is all we are saying and nothing more. Everything we here understand about God is contained in our understanding of the two words "not" and "material."

Considering the omnipotence of the supreme being, other positive notes emerge. A series of questions indicates what these must be.

Is an omnipotent being one that must be thought of as animate or inanimate—a living being or one that is inert?

If God must be thought of as a living being, must we not also think of God as knowing and as acting voluntarily, that is, as initiating action by willing it, not just reacting to being acted upon?

To be alive is to have more power than to be inert. Living things can do what the non-living cannot do.

In the realm of living things, to know is to have a vital power that is lacked by organisms incapable of knowing. Beings totally deprived of knowledge act or react blindly. Only those with knowledge can act intelligently, and can do what cannot be done by those without knowledge.

It not only follows that the supreme being must be a knowing and intelligent being, but also, being supreme, one that is omniscient and supremely intelligent. To be less than that would be less than supreme and omnipotent.

The difference between animate and inert, between knowing and not-knowing, and between intelligent and non-intelligent action, carries with it the difference between the voluntary and the non-voluntary. Only living, knowing, and intelligent beings can act voluntarily, can do as they will. Hence the supreme being is not only one that knows, but also one that wills.

The notes I have just added to our notion of God, drawn from the recognition that the supreme being must be thought of as omnipotent, are expressed in the same words that persons of religious faith use when they speak of the God they worship. They regard their deity as omnipotent and omniscient, as a living God, and as a God of whom they say, "Thy will be done, on earth as it is in Heaven."

These notes now added to our philosophical notion of God, which appear to be identical with attributes ascribed to God in sacred theology, are all positive in their significance. However, were we to use the words that express these notes in a strictly univocal sense, we would commit one of the most grievous of all theological mistakes. That mistake consists in adopting and embracing a completely anthropomorphic notion of God. When religious persons make this mistake, they cross the line that separates religion from superstition.

It is a mistake religious persons, undisciplined in philosophy, are inclined to make and do make frequently. Since we are here concerned with the bridge between philosophical thought about God and truly religious worship of God, not superstitious idolatry, let us try to prevent this mistake from being made on either side of the chasm.

When anything positive is said about God, it must be said analogically. It cannot be said univocally or literally. When, for example, we say that God *lives*, that God *knows*, and that God *wills*, we must never forget that we cannot use the words "lives," "knows," and "wills" in the same sense in which we apply these words to human beings or anything else. Divine life and human life are analogically alike-and-different, not univocally alike as your life and my life are.

What has just been said was pointed out earlier when we recognized that God's existence and the existence of individual things which are parts or components of the cosmos are analogically, not univocally, alike. One is the existence of an infinite, immaterial, immutable, independent, unconditioned, uncaused being; the other the existence of finite, material, mutable, dependent, conditioned, and caused beings. All that is common to the two is that both *exist in reality*, not merely as objects of thought. The likeness or *sameness* between them is integrally fused with all the *differences* mentioned.

In short, the negative notes that differentiate God from everything else we can think of infect the positive notes that allow us to think of God as somehow like other things we can think of.

Still another way of saying the same thing is even more radical. In the exact sense in which it can be truly affirmed that this or that individual thing really exists, God does *not* exist. If we could understand positively, not negatively, the exact sense in which it can be truly affirmed that God really exists, we would be compelled to say that nothing else really exists in that sense.

However, this is a supposition contrary to fact, for we can never come to understand positively the nature of the Divine existence. We are forever limited to making positive remarks that are at once negatively qualified: "God really exists, but not in the way that anything else really exists."

That constraint must be observed in every positive remark which we make about God: "God knows, but not in the way human beings know"—not by observation, reflection, or thought, not by perception or by reasoning, and so on. "God wills, but not in the way human beings will"; "God acts voluntarily, but not in the way human beings act voluntarily"; "God lives, but not in the way that human beings live"—not by interaction with the environment, not by the ingestion of nutriment, not by growing and declining, not as subject to health and disease, not as a result of being born, not as doomed to die.

Only by adding all the "nots" we can possibly think of every time we say anything positive about God, can we avoid the anthropomorphism that is both unphilosophical and irreligious. With this caution scrupulously and rigorously observed, we have made some advance toward discerning the affinity between the supreme being, as an object of philosophical thought, and the God worshiped by persons of religious faith.

Still observing this caution, we can add one more word that expresses a common note. In Western jurisprudence, we apply the word "person," in contradistinction to "thing," only to those living beings that have intellects capable of rational judgment and that have wills capable of free choice—in short, only to human beings. It is not enough to be alive in order to be a person. Brute animals are things, not persons, and are so regarded by the law.

The word "person" would appear to be applicable to the supreme being. If we were asked whether God is a person or a thing, we would certainly reply: "A person, not a thing." When religious individuals speak of a "personal God," and avoid being anthropomorphic in doing so, they understand no more than what is expressed by the negative phrase "not a thing." The Divine being and human beings are analogically alike as persons—alike with all the differences between infinite and finite, immaterial and material, and so on. Nevertheless, this very thin analogical likeness permits us to understand what is meant when religious persons declare that, of all terrestrial beings, only human beings are made in the image of God, for nothing else on earth is a person.

So far we have enriched our philosophical notion of God by adding a number of positive notes which appear to be entailed by the thought of a being that is the supreme being. To think of God as the supreme being requires us to think positively as well as negatively of God in respects implied by that notion, but always qualifying the additional positive notes by all the relevant negations.

Now let us consider the consequences that may derive from the cosmological argument, which enabled us to conclude that we have reasonable grounds for believing in God as exnihilator of the cosmos—*either preservatively*, by sustaining it in existence and preventing it from being reduced to nothingness, *or creatively*, by bringing it into existence out of nothing, *or both creatively and preservatively*. The consequences I have in mind relate to our notion of the supreme being as affected by the affirmation of God's existence as exnihilator.

We have already understood why the supreme being, having its existence from, through, and in itself, does not need to create the cosmos nor preserve it in existence. Having aseity, God's existence is totally unaffected by the existence of anything else. It cannot be enriched by the existence of anything else, or diminished by the non-existence of everything else.

That being so, God's creative and preservative action must be understood as an act of free choice. Since God is in no way necessitated to create or preserve the cosmos, but does so freely, we must ask: *Why?* To ask that question involves a degree of temerity we should seek to avoid. The Divine inscrutability should foreclose us from ever asking the reason why God does anything.

Nevertheless, when persons of religious faith say that "God is love," or, perhaps more accurately, that "God loves," they do so by virtue of their believing in the supreme being as the creator and preserver of the cosmos. To make something and to preserve it is an act of love, a benevolent overflowing of the maker's being into the being of something else.

If we understand that to exist is good (metaphysically, not morally, good), then perhaps we also can understand that the superabundant goodness which is one with the infinite existence of the supreme being overflows into the limited goodness and finite existence of the things that God brings into existence, and preserves in existence, when he creates and preserves the cosmos.

I must confess that I think we are on the most tenuous ground when, by such ratiocination, we add the positive note of "love" to our philosophical notion of God. To do so would, of course, bring that philosophical notion one step closer to the God of religious belief and worship; but from a strictly philosophical point of view, it is a much more tentative step than any we took earlier.

The remaining steps, which persons of religious faith would like us to take, I do not think philosophers can take at all, even in a tentative and heel-dragging manner. Religious persons believe that the creator and preserver of the cosmos acts lovingly and benevolently, and also that God possesses the perfection of moral goodness as well as the perfection of metaphysical goodness—that God is perfectly just and merciful.

If, as I said before, existence is good and non-existence is evil, metaphysically speaking, then we may have some ground for saying that the supreme being possesses the infinite goodness of infinite being. But this has no moral connotation whatsoever. It does not justify our speaking of God as just, or merciful, or as having any other moral quality that we regard as admirable and laudable in human beings.

This far we can go, and no further, with the exception of three concluding remarks.

The first concerns the note of omnipotence. This might have been added to our notion of God by reflection on the conclusion of the cosmological argument as well as by reflection on the notion of the supreme being. Anything less than an omnipotent being would not be a supreme being. It is also true that anything less than an omnipotent being could not make something out of nothing, or prevent something that exists from being reduced to absolute nothingness.

The second relates what has been said philosophically about God's aseity to a passage in the Old Testament that epitomizes the God worshipped in the three monotheistic religions of the West. It is the passage in which the hidden God, questioned by Moses concerning the nature of his divinity, replies: "I am who am." To be "he who is" is to have aseity—to have existence from, through, and in one's self. The God who revealed himself to the faithful in the Old Testament is, to this extent at least, the God of whom we have formed a philosophical notion and in whose existence we have found reasonable grounds to believe.

My third concluding comment responds to a question that readers of this book are likely to ask: Am I warranted, on rational grounds, in thinking of God as concerned with me—as caring about what I do and what happens to me in consequence? My answer follows.

To acknowledge God's omnipotence and omniscience, as we must, is to acknowledge that he knows and understands us better than we understand ourselves, that nothing about us is hidden from him, and that, within the bounds of possibility, he can do with us as he wills. However, to acknowledge this is not to be assured that God is concerned with our conduct or cares what happens to us.

The great dispute in the 18th century between the deists and the orthodox theologians was over the question whether the Deity that both affirmed was one who cared about his creatures, especially those of human kind, and caring, was concerned with the disposition of their lives—with answering their prayers, with helping them gratuitously even when they did not fully deserve such help.

Philosophical theology cannot resolve that dispute. In a state of ignorance about such matters, which is the state of the purely philosophical mind, we cannot say whether the God whose existence we have reason to affirm is indifferent to our fate or concerned with it. In that state of ignorance, the odds are fifty-fifty either way.

Faced with this option, the individual can resort to the reasoning involved in Pascal's wager, reasoning that led

Pascal to believe in a God that promised eternal rewards and punishments, not merely according to our merits but also in accordance with his benevolent grace. How each person weighs the alternatives that Pascal's wager places in the balance is, in the last analysis, not determined by reasoning alone, but by the direction of the individual will and by tendencies that rise from the deepest well-springs of the human spirit. In the words of Blaise Pascal, "*Le coeur a ses raisons que la raison ne connaît pas.*" The heart has its reasons that reason does not know.

CHAPTER 19

What Lies Ahead for the Reader

THE READER to whom this chapter is addressed is one who has just completed reading a book about God—perhaps the first book on that subject which he or she has ever read.

He or she may wish never to read another, may feel there is no need to read another, or, quite the contrary, may feel the need to read further in the literature of theology, and may have the time and will to do so.

Instead of the formalized bibliography that usually accompanies a treatise on an important subject, I would like to give readers who have both the interest and the inclination to delve further into the literature of theology a running account of the reading I have done over the course of a lifetime, but especially in the very recent past, while I was preparing to write this book.

Other readers who are themselves well acquainted with that literature, and may even be experts in it, may still have some interest in examining this running commentary on books or articles I have read, perhaps for the sake of appraising my competence in dealing with the problem of arguing for God's existence, certainly not for the sake of increasing their own competence to do so.

I will proceed in the following manner. First, I will mention the great and nearly great books, written up to the end of the 19th century, which have greatly influenced my thought. Second, I will enumerate books and articles of contemporary vintage from which I have profited, either by acquiring insights that I had not previously possessed or by having abiding insights of my own corroborated and confirmed. Third, I will mention other books and articles, or anthologies of articles, published in this century which, in one way or another, express views adverse to the views advanced in this book, or set forth criticisms and cautions that I have taken into account and tried to circumvent.

I will not comment on this third group of books or articles. The expert reader is fully cognizant of their criticisms and arguments and is in a position to judge whether I have met them. Inexpert readers need not concern themselves with this part of the literature until they have read much further in the books and articles cited in the two preceding sections. They will then require no help from me in making up their own minds on the matters in dispute.

Great Books of the Past

I have, of course, read most of the great books on the subject, and some of the nearly great. To discover the passages that I have pondered over long and often, readers need only turn to Chapter 29 in the *Syntopicon* attached to *Great*

Books of the Western World, published by Encyclopaedia Britannica, Inc. That is the chapter on God. There readers will find references to all the relevant passages, assembled under topics dealing with the notion of God, with belief in God, with arguments for or against the existence of God, with criticisms of attempts to prove God's existence, and so on. The principal authors cited under the various topics are Plato, Aristotle, Augustine, Aquinas, Bacon, Descartes, Spinoza, Pascal, Montaigne, Locke, Berkeley, Hume, Kant, Hegel, and Freud.

With respect to one of the great works in sacred theology that I have studied over the course of many years, the *Summa Theologica* of Thomas Aquinas, it might be helpful if I listed the passages in Part One that have been of special interest to me—affording insights that I have found nowhere else. They are as follows: Question 7, Articles 3–4, 12; Question 8, Article 2; Question 9, Article 2; Question 12, Article 12; Question 13, Articles 2, 5–6, 8–9, 11; Question 18, Article 3; Question 19, Article 4; Question 25, Articles 2–3, 5–6; Question 45, Articles 6, 8; Question 46, Article 2; Question 47, Article 1; Question 65, Articles 1, 3; Question 69, Article 2; Question 72, Article 1; Question 73, Article 1; Question 74, Articles 1–2; Question 104, Articles 1–4.

Other works by Aquinas, not included in *Great Books of the Western World*, should also be mentioned. They are his *Summa Contra Gentiles*, Book I, his *Disputed Questions on the Eternity of the World*, and his *Disputed Questions on the Power of God*.

Also not included in *Great Books of the Western World* are a number of other works that belong with the greats. They are: Augustine's *Answer to Skeptics*, Anselm's *Proslogium*, Maimonides' *The Guide for the Perplexed*, Leibnitz's *Discourse on Metaphysics* and *Theodicy*, Hume's *Dialogues Concerning Natural Religion*, Kant's *Religion Within*

the Limits of Reason Alone, J. S. Mill's "Theism" in his
Three Essays on Religion, and William James's *The Will to
Believe* and *The Sentiment of Rationality*.

The foregoing enumeration of works written up to the
end of the 19th century is not intended to be exhaustive. I
have merely listed important works that I have found it
profitable to study, in addition to the works included in
Great Books of the Western World.

Contemporary Books and Articles

I turn now to the second category of works that have
influenced my thinking. These are all books or articles that
have been written and published in this century. From the
study of them, I have profited by acquiring new insights or
by having insights already possessed confirmed and corroborated. I have listed the works alphabetically by author.
In a few cases I have cited pages of special significance to
me. In all cases, I have given the bibliographical informa-
tion that readers may need in order to locate or obtain the
work mentioned.

Clarke, Bowman L. *Language and Natural Theology*. The Hague:
    Mouton & Co., 1966.
Clarke, W. Norris. "How the Philosopher Can Give Meaning to
    Language About God." In *The Idea of God*, E. H. Mad-
    den, R. Handy, and M. Farber, eds. Springfield, Ill.:
    Charles C. Thomas, 1968.
De Lubac, Henri. *The Discovery of God*. New York: P. J.
    Kenedy and Sons, 1960, especially chapters 1–3.
Eddington, Sir Arthur Stanley. *Science and the Unseen World*.
    London: Allen and Unwin, 1929.
Garrigou-Lagrange, R. *God, His Existence and Nature*. St.
    Louis: St. Louis University Press, 1934, especially Ap-
    pendix.
Gilson, Etienne. *Being and Some Philosophers*. Toronto: Pon-
    tifical Institute of Mediaeval Studies, 1949, especially
    pp. 160–182.

———. *Christianity and Philosophy*. London: Sheed and Ward, 1939, especially pp. 77–102.

———. "The Idea of God and the Difficulties of Atheism." In *The Great Ideas Today 1969*, M. J. Adler and R. M. Hutchins, eds. Chicago: Encyclopaedia Britannica, Inc., 1969.

Gunn, James E. "Observations in Cosmology: The Shape of Space and Totality of Time." In *The Great Ideas Today 1979*, M. J. Adler, ed. Chicago: Encyclopaedia Britannica, Inc., 1979.

Hawking, Stephen W. "The Limits of Space and Time." In *The Great Ideas Today 1979*. M. J. Adler, ed. Chicago: Encyclopaedia Britannica, Inc., 1979.

Heisenberg, Werner. *Philosophic Problems of Nuclear Science*. New York: Pantheon Books, Inc., 1952.

———. *Physics and Philosophy: The Revolution in Modern Science*. New York: Harper & Bros., 1958.

Jastrow, Joseph. *God and the Astronomers*. New York: W. W. Norton & Co., 1978.

McInerny, Ralph. "Can God Be Named by Us?" *The Review of Metaphysics*, vol. 32, no. 1, September 1978.

Maritain, Jacques. *Approaches to God*. New York: Harper & Bros., 1954.

———. *Range of Reason*. New York: Charles Scribner's Sons, 1952, especially chapters 7–8.

Mascall, E. L. *Existence and Analogy*. London: Longmans, Green and Co., 1949, especially pp. 74–75, 86–89, 124, 143–147.

———. *He Who Is*. London: Longmans, Green and Co., 1943.

Murray, John Courtney. *The Problem of God: Yesterday and Today*. New Haven, Conn.: Yale University Press, 1964, especially chapter 2.

Newman, John Henry. *An Essay in Aid of a Grammar of Assent*. London: Longmans, Green & Co., 1939 (first edition, London, 1870).

Royce, Josiah. *The Conception of God: An Address Before the Union*. New York: Macmillan Publishing Company, 1902 (first edition, Berkeley, Calif., 1895).

Sillem, Edward. *Ways of Thinking About God*. New York: Sheed and Ward, 1961, especially pp. 118–133, 136–139, 160–165.

Taylor, Alfred Edward. *Does God Exist?* New York: Macmillan Publishing Company, 1947 (first edition, 1945).

Toulmin, Stephen. "Arthur Koestler's Theodicy." *Encounter*, vol. 52, no. 2, February 1979.

Weinberg, Steven. *The First Three Minutes: A Modern View of the Origin of the Universe.* New York: Basic Books, Inc., 1977.

Wolter, Allan B. "An Oxford Dialogue on Language and Metaphysics I." *The Review of Metaphysics*, vol. 31, no. 4, June 1978.

————. "An Oxford Dialogue on Language and Metaphysics II." *The Review of Metaphysics*, vol. 32, no. 2, December 1978.

Adverse Views

Finally, I come to the third category of works that I have examined and in which I have found views contrary to my own, and arguments against or criticisms of views that I hold. I have paid attention to these adverse arguments and criticisms and I have tried my best to surmount or circumvent the difficulties they raise.

Ayer, A. J. "Theology as Meaningless." In *The Existence of God*, J. H. Hick, ed. New York: Macmillan Publishing Company, 1964.

Findley, J. N. "Can God's Existence Be Disproved?" In *New Essays in Philosophical Theology*, A. Flew and A. MacIntyre, eds. New York: Macmillan Publishing Company, 1955.

Flew, Antony G. *God and Philosophy.* New York: Harcourt, Brace and World, 1966.

Flew, Antony G., and D. M. MacKinnon. "Creation." In *New Essays in Philosophical Theology*, A. Flew and A. MacIntyre, eds. New York: Macmillan Publishing Company, 1955.

Hartshorne, Charles. *Anselm's Discovery: A Re-Examination of the Ontological Proof for God's Existence.* LaSalle, Ill.: Open Court Publishing Company, 1965.

————. *A Natural Theology for Our Time*. LaSalle, Ill.: Open Court Publishing Company, 1967.

Hick, J. H., and A. C. McGill, eds. *The Many-Faced Argument*. New York: Macmillan Publishing Company, 1967.

Madden, E. H., R. Handy, and M. Farber, eds. *The Idea of God*. Springfield, Ill.: Charles C. Thomas, 1968, especially chapters 2–8, 13–16.

Malcolm, Norman. "A Contemporary Discussion [of the Ontological Argument]." In *The Existence of God*, J. H. Hick, ed. New York: Macmillan Publishing Company, 1964.

Matson, Wallace I. *The Existence of God*. Ithaca, N.Y.: Cornell University Press, 1965.

Plantinga, Alvin. *God and Other Minds: A Study of the Rational Justification of Belief in God*. Ithaca, N.Y.: Cornell University Press, 1967.

————. *The Nature of Necessity*. New edition. New York: Oxford University Press, 1978.

————, ed. *The Ontological Argument from St. Anselm to Contemporary Philosophers*. New York: Doubleday & Company, 1965.

Russell, Bertrand, and F. C. Copleston. "A Debate on the Existence of God." In *The Existence of God*, J. H. Hick, ed. New York: Macmillan Publishing Company, 1964.

Smart, J. J. C. "Metaphysics, Logic and Theology," "The Existence of God," and "Theology and Falsification." In *New Essays in Philosophical Theology*, A. Flew and A. MacIntyre, eds. New York: Macmillan Publishing Company, 1955.

Wisdom, John. "The Modes of Thought and the Logic of God." In *The Existence of God*, J. H. Hick, ed. New York: Macmillan Publishing Company, 1964.

ABOUT THE AUTHOR

MORTIMER J. ADLER is the chairman of Encyclopaedia Britannica's board of editors, director of the Institute for Philosophical Research in Chicago, and a senior associate of the Aspen Institute for Humanistic Studies, of which he was one of the founders. He is the author of the well-known *How to Read a Book*, *Philosopher at Large*, his intellectual autobiography, and *Aristotle for Everybody*; and co-editor, with Charles Van Doren, of *Great Treasury of Western Thought*, declared the "reference book of 1977" by the American Library Association.

Heartwarming Books
of
Faith and Inspiration

☐	20376	**CROSSROADS** by L. Jaworski/D. Schneider	$2.95
☐	14725	**PILGRIMS REGRESS** C. S. Lewis	$2.50
☐	20299	**MERTON: A BIOGRAPHY**	$3.95
☐	20464	**LOVE AND LIVING** Thomas Merton	$3.50
☐	20618	**A SEVERE MERCY** Sheldon Vanauken	$2.95
☐	01184	**HE WAS ONE OF US: THE LIFE OF JESUS OF NAZARETH** Rien Poortvliet	$9.95
☐	20784	**POSITIVE PRAYERS FOR POWER-FILLED LIVING** Robert H. Schuller	$2.50
☐	14732	**HOW CAN I FIND YOU, GOD?** Marjorie Holmes	$2.50
☐	20794	**THE BIBLE HISTORY** Werner Keller	$3.95
☐	20551	**THE GREATEST MIRACLE IN THE WORLD** Og Mandino	$2.50
☐	20143	**THE GREATEST SECRET IN THE WORLD** Og Mandino	$2.50
☐	14515	**CHRIST COMMISSION** Og Mandino	$2.75
☐	01303	**THE 1980'S COUNTDOWN TO ARMAGEDDON** Hal Lindsey	$6.95
☐	20613	**THE GREATEST SALESMAN IN THE WORLD** Og Mandino	$2.50
☐	14971	**I'VE GOT TO TALK TO SOMEBODY, GOD** Marjorie Holmes	$2.50
☐	12444	**BORN AGAIN** Charles Colson	$2.50
☐	14840	**A GRIEF OBSERVED** C. S. Lewis	$2.50
☐	22623	**TWO FROM GALILEE** Marjorie Holmes	$2.95
☐	20727	**LIGHTHOUSE** Eugenia Price	$2.95
☐	22502	**THE LATE GREAT PLANET EARTH** Hal Lindsey	$2.95

BANTAM NEW AGE BOOKS

Bantam New Age Books are for all those interested in reflecting on life today and life as it may be in the future. This important new imprint features stimulating works in fields from biology and psychology to philosophy and the new physics.

☐	13578	**THE DANCING WU LI MASTERS:** An Overview of the New Physics Gary Zukav	$3.95
☐	14131	**THE FIRST THREE MINUTES** Steven Weinberg	$2.95
☐	13470	**LIFETIDE** Lyall Watson	$3.50
☐	12478	**MAGICAL CHILD** Joseph Chilton Pearce	$3.50
☐	13406	**THE MEDUSA AND THE SNAIL** Lewis Thomas	$2.95
☐	13724	**MIND AND NATURE:** A Necessary Unity Gregory Bateson	$3.50
☐	20322	**HEALTH FOR THE WHOLE PERSON** James Gordon	$3.95
☐	20708	**ZEN/MOTORCYCLE MAINTENANCE** Robert Pirsig	$3.95
☐	20693	**THE WAY OF THE SHAMAN** Michael Harner	$3.95
☐	10949	**TO HAVE OR TO BE** Fromm	$2.95
☐	14821	**IN THE SHINING MOUNTAINS** David Thomson	$3.95
☐	14526	**FOCUSING** Eugene Gendlin	$3.50
☐	13972	**LIVES OF A CELL** Lewis Thomas	$2.95
☐	14206	**TAO OF PHYSICS** Fritjof Capra	$3.95
☐	14912	**KISS SLEEPING BEAUTY GOODBYE** M. Kolbenschlag	$3.95